CULT MOVIES IN SIXTY SECONDS

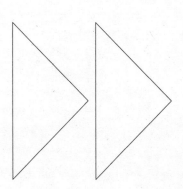

CULT MOVIES
IN
SIXTY SECONDS

THE BEST FILMS IN THE WORLD
IN LESS THAN A MINUTE

Soren McCarthy

ff

For my mum and dad
whose constant subtle grace
taught me
subtext

First published in Great Britain in 2003 by Fusion Press,
a division of Satin Publications Ltd.
101 Southwark Street
London SE1 0JF
UK
info@visionpaperbacks.co.uk
www.visionpaperbacks.co.uk
Publisher: Sheena Dewan

A catalogue record for this book is available from the British Library.

ISBN: 1-904132-16-2

2 4 6 8 10 9 7 5 3 1

Cover and page design by ok?design
Printed and bound in the UK by Mackays of Chatham Limited.

Contents

▶ Acknowledgements

Thanks to Charlotte Cole, Carmen Baumgardner Fox, Joe Bob Briggs, Hank Boland, Stephen Colbert, Kelli Clendion, Paul Chart, Rich Fulcher, Joanna Gleason, Michael McCarthy, Richard Metzger, Tom Purcell, Leslie Rosenberg, Brian Stack, Carla San Diego, Chris Sarandon, Rob Sell, Nick and Joanna Vergoth, Matt Lageman and Kirsten Olsen-Lageman, The Akron Civic Theater, Video Archives Los Angeles, The Cedar Lee Theater Cleveland, TLA Video NYC, Video Stop NYC, Facets Video Chicago and especially The Donald and Donna McCarthy Foundation for Starving Writers.

INTRODUCTION

To truly enjoy a cult film, you have to be inclined towards the obscure. You are someone who has a favourite out-of-the-way restaurant and a bargain jacket found in a charity shop. Or favourite designer that no one has heard of. These movies are not defined by box-office earnings, nor by critical acclaim. Popularity rarely comes into the equation. This book seeks to be true to the free spirit of cult films by examining, advocating, chiding, but invariably appreciating films. A great film is not defined by the size of the audience, so much as the nature of the response it provokes.

I am a writer and actor based in New York. As someone who has worked in both obscure and mass mediums, I know what it is like to get critique, and applaud anyone who puts themselves 'out there' artistically.

I came to love movies at a young age, at the period when home video rentals were revolutionising the film industry. Suddenly access was available to all, and even a kid like me from Akron, Ohio could get a video copy of *Stranger than Paradise* (1984), a film by Jim Jarmusch, another kid from Akron, Ohio which would never actually play in an Akron, Ohio cinema.

Like many medium-sized cities my hometown also had a second run arthouse cinema. The Akron Civic Theater was a gigantic 2,000 person auditorium from the vaudeville era. A theatre and a cinema, it had an ornate domed ceiling with light fixtures meant to resemble stars, upon which moving clouds were projected. It avoided demolition and a foundation kept it a working theatre by showing second run films. After home video killed much of the second run market, they switched to cult, art and special-event films. Provided I volunteered as an usher, I was allowed to see all the movies as often as I liked for free. I got to see the European art films of Federico Fellini, Wim Wenders, Francoise Truffaut and Werner Herzog, and all before I was 15 years old.

What I enjoyed as much as the films was the experience a live audience could offer. I liked the shared experience of a film in an auditorium setting, and watching the audiences as much as the films. I loved the willingness of strangers to discuss a film with one another. It was an opportunity to encounter like-minded people. (This was before internet chat, when a 'discussion' required an actual 'room'.) A film like *Harold and Maude* could be counted on to draw a large audience for every showing. I recognised regulars who never missed a revival of this cult classic. But there was no easy way to categorise these fans as a demographic (in terms of ages, races, orientations etc). They just liked it, and could recognise a great film. In an age of concentrated marketing and 'target audience segmentation', I found this refreshing.

I developed this book based on an entirely imperfect consensus. I spoke to lay people, film aficionados, independent theatre owners and video store clerks. I was amazed and pleased at how forthcoming people were in naming their own cult favourites. At one point, while on a church retreat, someone asked my mother about my cult film project, which lead to such an involved group discussion that they scrapped all their 'getting to know you' exercises and simply chatted about their personal favourite cult films and why they considered them so. Three days later I received a stack of notebook pages with the cult favourites of 50 middle-aged Christians from Ohio. To my surprise the bawdy and shocking John Waters film *Pink Flamingos* showed up very often. But then, it's a liberal denomination.

We each have our list. Those few movies that have touched something in us, for which we have an enduring affection. Each list is hugely indicative of a person. You may open a conversation with a stranger by asking 'What do you do?' or 'Where did you got to school?' But if you want to watch someone really blossom, ask them about their top five cult films.

Naming their cult favourites, people don't find it necessary to justify their preferences, but it helps if they do. Nevertheless, for this book, the manner in which I attempt to identify a cult has everything to do with the following components:

ENDURANCE – RESONANCE – AFFECTION
Repeated viewing does not diminish a cult film's appeal. Often these are those an enthusiast will go back to throughout their lives, and still find the themes and ideas meaningful. Such movies have a resonance that extends to broad audiences, both demographically and geographically. The affection they incite is not just liking, but passion and even devotion.

TECHNICAL CRAFTSMANSHIP – SCOPE – ORIGINALITY
These movies often exude the technical prowess of their creators. A cult film dazzles us with the richness of its references (to other films, to popular or high culture or even just to itself). It may shatter all existing genres: a truly cult film can be said to define a genre, a place and a time.

None of the above components are necessary for a film to be cult. But combinations of them should be enough. I hope.

While I differentiate 'cult' from 'commercial success' or 'critical successes', the definitions will not be entirely mutually exclusive. Some films may be commercial successes and cult films (*Apocalypse Now*). Some may be big budget films that were initially commercial failures (*Blade Runner*). Some may be critical but not commercial successes (such as Warren Beatty's *Reds*).

Other films garner passionate followings within very specific and defined groups. For example, the film *Network* is a cult favourite among journalists and media industry workers. *Valley of the Dolls* is a gospel among drag queens. And *This Is Spinal Tap* can be recited nearly word-for-word by almost everyone who has ever worked with or performed as a musician.

Sometimes even a huge mainstream film has a sub group of particularly devoted followers. *Star Wars* may be the most popular film of all time, but within its general popularity is a hard-core of devotees. Case in point: a 2001 census in Australia revealed 70,509 people wrote 'Jedi' or Jedi-related answers when asked 'Religion'. While a well-orchestrated prank, it certainly blurs the literal definition of 'cult' film. While I think this is a fascinating incident, so much ink has already been pressed on *Star Wars* I felt it more practical to devote entries to lesser-known films.

Conversely, enormous passion attached to a film can be disproportionate to the number of viewers; ie very big love from a very small crowd. There are films so rarely seen they are more myth than masterpiece, particularly controversial films more often discussed than actually viewed. I illustrated this by including the film *The Day the Clown Cried*. This movie, an unreleased yet infamous opus by writer/director/star Jerry Lewis, has been viewed by less than 30 people. Yet, for many people intrigued by its inaccessibility and the notoriety generated by its guarded suppression, it is still a point of fascination. It's become more cult than film, so it's the *61st movie in this book. Don't agree? Good!

There are films included here about which you will undoubtedly argue that they don't deserve the status of 'cult'. Likewise I hope you will think of some personal favourites whose absence annoys you. In doing so, you are well on your way to defining your own cult criteria and building your personal list. I invite you to email your feedback to cultmovies60@yahoo.co.uk. I'd love to be introduced to, or rediscover, a whole new batch of favourite cult films – it may even write a second volume.

▶▶

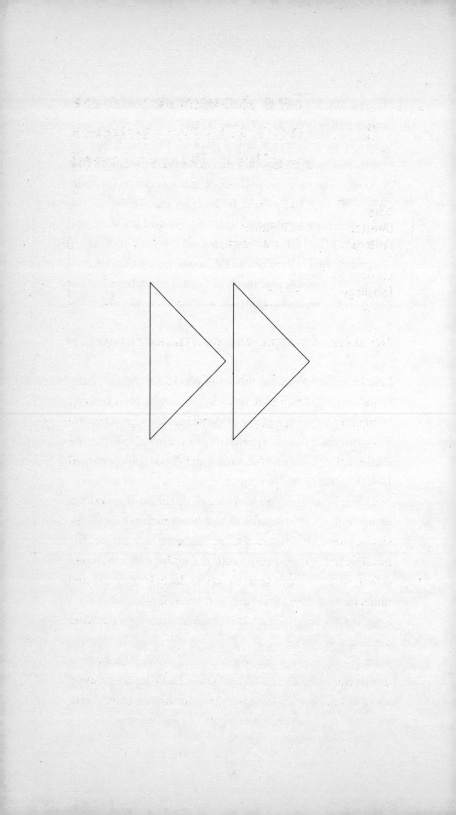

THE ADVENTURES OF BUCKAROO BANZAI ACROSS THE 8TH DIMENSION!

Date:	1984
Director:	W.D. Richter
Writer(s):	Earl Mac Rauch
Runtime(s):	103 minutes
Country:	US
Language:	English

NO MATTER WHERE YOU GO, THERE YOU ARE.

Like so many cult films, this 1984 production was initially considered a box-office failure. Its cult popularity grew by word of mouth and the advocacy of American ubercritic Pauline Kael. Essentially it's the typical story of a scientist/rock 'n' roll musician/brain surgeon/samurai who fights evil aliens named John from the eighth dimension.

This is a brilliant and lively spoof of the sci-fi superhero genre. Visually and aurally rich, it bears multiple viewings, yielding fresh surprises each time. The retro-techno look, the non-linear alien spacecraft and the entire cast's deadpan delivery of gee-whiz material blend effortlessly. It's excessive and understated at the same time and its underlying silliness is engaging, even to adult sensibilities. And it has Jeff Goldblum dressed as a cowboy.

An opening story background crawl, a la *Star Wars*, informs us that Buckaroo Banzai (Peter Weller) had a Japanese father and a US mother, and is expert in neurosurgery, martial arts, particle physics and music. His colleagues, all 'hard rocking scientists', back him up in a band called The Hong Kong Cavaliers. He also has his own quasi boy-scout organisation: The Blue Blazers.

The film opens with team Banzai preparing to launch a rocket car in the desert flats. Unfortunately, test pilot Banzai is missing, off recruiting a top surgeon (Jeff Goldblum). Once the doctor agrees (in the midst of performing an operation), Buckaroo enquires somewhat unexpectedly, 'Can you sing?' Goldblum's character responds, 'A little ... I can dance.'

Soon after, Banzai manages to show up at the test site dressed in a black, Ninja-style fire suit. The jet car is launched at break-neck speed directly at the mountain. A blue beam from the car zaps the mountain and, rather than crash, the car appears to be absorbed into the mountain. It briefly enters 'the eighth dimension' while travelling through the mountain's mass. The hero and his jet then rematerialize on the other side of the mountain, unharmed.

The rest of the film involves an alien species, called Lectroids, who inhabit the eighth dimension. Buckaroo's trespass enables the Lectroids and their inter-galactic race war to spill over into our dimension. Black Lectroids, who appear to humans as Rastafarians, are good, while the bad Red Lectroids appear as typical white males.

The Red Lectroids (all incidentally named John) are attempting a world takeover through a front corporation ('Yoyodyne Propulsion') and the help of mad Doctor Lizardo (John Lithgow, whose performance steals this movie). Christopher Lloyd and Dan Hedaya also turn up in hilarious performances as two of the aliens (John Bigboote and John Gomez respectively).

When the Black Lectroids discover that arch criminal Dr. Lizardo is on the loose on Earth, they threaten to wipe out the entire planet. They give Buckaroo 24 hours to capture or kill him lest they be forced to annihilate the earth.

Meanwhile, Buckaroo's love interest is a 'lost soul' named Penny (Ellen Barkin), introduced attempting suicide at a Hong Kong Cavaliers club date. She also happens to be his deceased wife's long-lost twin sister ...

Confused? That's okay. It even opens with the sense that you've walked into a movie halfway through. It is so rich with quick, odd bits of detail that you sense that each hints at a richer story. Likewise just enough of the characters' back-stories are revealed to pique our interest. The only way to pack so much into a 102-minute movie, is to simply discard structure and continuity. It's not that it is disjointed; it's more that it trusts you to be on it, or at least interested enough to work through any confusion. It is smart, energetic, infectious, truly odd fun.

I first saw it on video release in 1984 and, for reasons I still cannot explain, I watched it five times in a single weekend. I think much of sci-fi is dependant on heroes who embody a specific ideal. The attraction of the Buckaroo character is that he embodies the ultimate fantasy: of simultaneously being everything at once.

The ending credits alert the audience to watch out for the sequel, 'Buckaroo Banzai versus The World Crime League'. I only wish it had been produced.

▶▶

Date:	1988
Director:	Katsuhiro Ôtomo
Writer(s):	Katsuhiro Ôtomo, Izô Hashimoto
Runtime(s):	124 minutes
Country:	Japan
Language:	Japanese

NEO-TOKYO IS ABOUT TO E.X.P.L.O.D.E.

The entire genre of Japanese Anime is a cult unto itself. I hesitate in limiting the inclusion of Anime entries to a thousand films, let alone one. Anime's following is so passionate that no selection is going to be good enough for its devotees. So before they come home from their schools/jobs at video/hobby/ comic-book stores or jet-propulsion laboratories and get on the Internet to issue a Satanic Verses style fatwa, understand that I comprehend this. As no list would be complete, I simply give you the undisputed classic: *Akira*.

Basically it's an animated Hong Kong action film in a sci-fi setting. Set in a post-holocaust Japan, a repressed society begins to uncoil, governmental psiops programs are in progress, and two motorcycle gang members and an escaped young boy become the catalysts for a new world order.

Gang leader Kaneda and his friend Tetsuo battle a rival gang. Tetsuo is seriously injured and taken to a military hospital, where he becomes the subject of a secret army experiment in ESP that renders him able to destroy anything by sheer will.

Escaping from the hospital and on the verge of insanity, Tetsuo sweeps through Tokyo armed with his supernatural power. It's up to Kaneda, his rebel friend Kei and a trio of 'psionics' to stop Tetsuo and prevent the destruction of the world.

The plot can be too complicated for its own good, becoming somewhat entangled in the ideas it is juggling, with too many subplots and minor dramas to maintain focus. If you want to fully appreciate *Akira*, I suggest you watch it at least three times so you can fully piece together all the elements.

The film is notable because the director (Katsuhiro Ôtomo) also created the comic on which it is based. This rarely happens. Some of the convolutions in the plot may have arisen from the challenge of condensing one's own 38-volume manga into a 2-hour film.

The animation is stunning – burning from the neon of Neo-Tokyo, where giant advertising hoardings float over huge skyscrapers and bustling street markets while motorbikes paint streaks of light across the motorways. It positively drips with light and colour, most notably in the film's unforgettable opening ten minutes. *Akira* is the true spirit of cyber-punk – anarchic, intense, dark and virtually crackling with sheer energy. One of the things that stands out in this movie is the detail. The texture on buildings, realistic lighting effects and constant movement in the background make the film extremely atmospheric. A superb soundtrack by Shoji Yamashiro reinforces the effect.

The characters move fluidly and realistically. It sounds like pure geek snobbery to suggest that a dubbed version of animation could be inferior, but if one watches the subtitled version of the film, the speech actually matches the characters' mouth movement. Likewise, elements of dialogue and emotional subtext really are lost in the bare-bones translations.

Akira is a very influential film. It brought the anime genre into the mainstream. It had a deep stylistic influence not just on animated action features, but also on sci-fi generally. The resemblance between *Akira* and *The Matrix* is not coincidental. The creators of *The Matrix* (1999), the Wachowski brothers, have enthusiastically cited *Akira* as an influence.

APOCALYPSE NOW

Date:	1979
Director:	Francis Ford Coppola
Writer(s):	John Milius, Francis Ford Coppola and Michael Herr (narration)
Runtime(s):	153 minutes, 202 minutes (USA, Redux version)
Country:	USA
Language:	English, French, Vietnamese, Khmer

I WAS GOING TO THE
WORST PLACE IN THE WORLD
AND I DIDN'T EVEN KNOW IT YET.

This film is a glorious risk. It's opera, it's Shakespeare and it's the cinematic equivalent of a novel. The audacity of vision, and the cost overruns to achieve it, represent a gamble that independent filmmakers rarely approximate. Timely in its releases, and enduring in popularity for 20 years, *Apocalypse Now* is a series of overwhelming images underscoring complex themes.

How is it that a big budget classic can attain cult status? Some films can attain mainstream popularity while maintaining a devoted cadre of aficionados. *Apocalypse Now* carries a certain resonance in American pop culture. Even its complicated production history has achieved near mythical status, spawning a popular documentary about the making of the film, *Hearts of Darkness* (1991). Further, the excitement that surrounded the *Apocalypse Now Redux* (2001) release affirmed its cult status, with a devoted audience expanding their experience of the film.

Adapted from Joseph Conrad's *Heart Of Darkness*, *Apocalypse Now* is transplanted into the chaos of the Vietnam War circa

1969. It opens with The Door's 'The End' playing over scenes of a napalmed jungle. Captain Benjamin L. Willard (Martin Sheen) of US Army Intelligence is handed a mission in Saigon. A renegade officer, Colonel Walter E. Kurtz (Marlon Brando), is conducting a personal war with his own army outside the boundaries of operations in Cambodia. Kurtz is worshiped like a god and is operating 'beyond the pale of any acceptable human conduct' and, as General R. Corman (G.D. Spradlin) informs Willard: 'His command must be terminated. Kurtz must be terminated. With extreme prejudice.' Willard will have to track down Kurtz by riding a small boat upriver with a few soldiers, and then kill him. Willard receives a long dossier on Kurtz from which he familiarises himself with the Colonel's background during the boat trip.

Along the way, he has many encounters that make him realise the insanity and horror of Vietnam. The helicopter raid sequence is perhaps the best fifteen or twenty minutes ever committed to film. An atrocity committed against a Vietnamese fishing boat is reminiscent of My Lai.

> **The best equipped army cannot defeat a nation armed with the deepest conviction and no army can defeat an opponent who understands them completely.**
>
> *The Art of War* by Sun Tzu

What separates *Apocalypse Now* from other notable Vietnam films (*Full Metal Jacket* (1987), *The Boys in Company C* (1978), *Platoon* (1986)) is the conviction within it to convey the experience of the war. It does this, not through realistic portrayals, but by inducing a surreal experience that conveys the surreal circumstances – just as the madness of colonial adventurism was conveyed in *Heart of Darkness*. The horror and savagery lie not in the jungle, but in American culture. In this regard the movie is both beautiful and horrific, surreal yet authentic. Such strong elements that normally might eclipse one another are reconciled in balance, and therein lies Coppola's artistry. This is the license of any 2-hour-plus artistic endeavour. What the film fails to provide in clarity and purpose, two elements absent from the war itself, makes it a better film.

As well as the insanity of war, the idea of man's descent into madness is at the forefront. Willard originally sees reason in killing Kurtz, but as he encounters the horrors of Vietnam he begins to understand Kurtz, and almost becomes him.

The performances are remarkable. I know what you are thinking … Brando playing an egomaniacal madman? Yes! Dennis Hopper portraying a man out of his mind? Somehow he found the character. The Kurtz character is inextricably linked to Brando. Dennis Hopper is not just a photojournalist or just a sleazy sycophant – he is the insane harlequin.

Martin Sheen's restrained performance perfectly fits the emotionally disrupted Captain Willard, and his voiceover does not feel obtrusive or grow boring. It is necessary for such an internal character to experience revelations as he does, which reveal his respect for Kurtz. Willard has already carried out 'assassinations' for the Government and is, in his own way, almost a war victim; he is alive, but he feels soulless, and the perspective needed for a regular life seems lost for ever – particularly because of a divorce from his wife, for which he blames the greater part on himself. A beautiful sympathy develops in Willard as he researches Kurtz. The journey itself is a necessary primer for the confrontation. Travelling upriver against the backdrop of so much horror, Willard begins to identify with Kurtz. The intimacy becomes more reciprocal as we realise that Kurtz has been sizing up Willard's worthiness as his own assassin.

Robert Duvall appears in one of the most fascinating cameos in cinema as Colonel Kilgore. If there can be such a thing as a 'cult performance', this is it. The famous sequence where he plays Wagner's *Ride of the Valkyries* during an air raid is an immortal cinema moment. The same for his infamous quote, 'I love the smell of napalm in the morning ... It smells like ... victory.'

When the surf-obsessed Kilgore takes a beachhead and declares righteously that 'Charlie don't surf!', it is such a brilliant encapsulation of the American notion that Vietnam has been wasted on the Vietnamese and, by extension, 'destroying in order to save' becomes justified. An additional scene involving Kilgore reinserted in *Apocalypse Now Redux*, actually detracts from the mystique of the character.

The original *Apocalypse Now* editor Walter Murch restored 49 minutes to the film for the 2001 re-release. He is a frequent Coppola collaborator and had previously recut *Godfather I* and *II* to create a single chronology.

The most significant change in the new edit is the addition of the 'French plantation scene', a long and dreamy interlude that was to be the last stop for Captain Willard and the crew before encountering Colonel Kurtz. Allegedly, Coppola and Murch cut the scene in the original release because they felt it stalled the narrative just short of the climax: they were right. The ghost of French failure foreshadows America's fate, and illustrates the arrogance in failing to recognise a cautionary example. But the scenes are mostly didactic, illustrating a wizened French perspective on Vietnam, and underscoring the themes of colonial folly from *Heart of Darkness*.

The other additions are minor, but extraneous. Another episode involving a group of Playboy bunnies is needlessly extended into a subplot. A new scene in which Kurtz reads to Willard from *Time* magazine may further emphasise Kurtz's grim lucidity, but it merely puts a fine point on issues that have already been worked over elsewhere.

Hearts of Darkness, the documentary made by Coppola's wife about the making of the film, is almost a cult film in its own right. Authenticity and extreme characters rarely intersect as vividly as they do here. The filming itself was a remarkable undertaking. Endless problems, including a typhoon that destroyed most of the sets, difficulties with the authorities of the Philippines (where the film was shot) and personal problems with the actors and the crew, brought the costs sky high and the shooting process from the scheduled six weeks up to 16 months. Initially Harvey Keitel played Captain Willard. They filmed for six weeks before Coppola instituted the change. Eight months into production, Martin Sheen had a near fatal heart attack. Coppola himself at the end was almost physically, financially and psychologically devastated.

The level of interest in *Apocalypse Now* affirms it as a source of hardcore fascination and cult status among some. The *Apocalypse Now Redux* re-release provides extended ruminations on certain themes. A good film in its own right, the documentary *Hearts of Darkness* is at the very least a vital companion piece to the original film.

▶▶

BAD BOY BUBBY

Date:	1993
Director:	Rolf de Heer
Writer(s):	Rolf de Heer
Runtime(s):	112 minutes
Country:	Australia
Language:	English

ALL HE NEEDS IS LOVE.

As a rule, Hollywood portrays the mentally disabled as quaint, likeable, quirky and entirely benign people who occasionally say the wisest things. No wait, I'm thinking of Australians. Anyway, if you want to watch both conventions refreshingly shattered, see the Australian Indy legend *Bad Boy Bubby*.

It may seem like a Francis Bacon painting come to life, and you may come very, very close to switching it off. Do yourself a favour and give it five minutes, and another five, and another. After the first twenty minutes of horrified fascination, you'll appreciate the pay off.

'Bubby' (Nicholas Hope) has been locked up in his room for all his 35 years and used as a sex toy by his mother. He eventually gets out into the real world and discovers it can't be any worse. Like a darkly inverted Chauncey Gardner from *Being There*, Bubby is a blank slate thrust into the world, attempting to interpret it from a limited and damaged perspective. It's like Plato's cave in a modern twisted world: Bubby is a master mimic and can only parrot back phrases he has heard.

The series of vignettes connect less to form a plot as a journey of discovery. Much of his journey involves the coincidences, symbolism and overtly self-aware characters that only surface in low-budget 'message films'. And yet limitations aside, it is a very unique and brave film that manages to say a lot. Bubby encounters technology, theology, music and sex in a whirlwind. He is not a passive observer. He actively wants to participate, touch and connect with all he sees. Although sometimes to his detriment, this drive ultimately serves him.

So many Hollywood actors fail to give up the vanity necessary to do a disabled role, precisely because they are doing the role out of vanity. Nicholas Hope is excellent as Bubby. He is convincingly awkward. The role is sympathetic enough to give us permission to laugh at some of his choices. I admired the use of disabled actors, and found those scenes both non-patronising and refreshingly honest.

As the film involves a character entering the world for the first time, you will forgive it if some of the dialogue is didactic. The band member's monologue regarding the history of cultures 'cling-filming' ('plastic wrap' for our North American readers) each other is a nice distillation of world history. It's a simple explanation and disturbingly true.

Hollywood approaches all subjects in a manner that affirms society overall: it allows challenges to our sense of well-being only as a means of dismissing them. *Bad Boy Bubby* declares that society has a great deal for which to account. A character delivers a monologue in which he states we must, 'Think god out of existence, it is our duty to insult him, strike me down if you dare to, you tyrant, you non-existent fraud. It is our duty to think god out of existence, because then and only then do we take full responsibility for who we are!' Agree or not, I will support any film that trusts me enough to draw my own conclusions.

It's all a matter of taste. Everyone will find something in it disturbing and affirming in turns. If you share Bubby's fascination with 'Great tits ... big whoppers of 'em' you'll enjoy much of it. Whereas if you are a cat lover, you might find it difficult in places. But by the time you reach the ending with Lisa Gerard beautifully interpreting Handel's 'Largo' you'll mostly remember the good.

▶▶

BADLANDS

Date:	1973
Director:	Terrence Malick
Writer(s):	Terrence Malick
Runtime(s):	95 minutes
Country:	US
Language:	English

IN 1959 A LOT OF PEOPLE WERE KILLING TIME.
KIT AND HOLLY WERE KILLING PEOPLE.

It seems every creatively bankrupt director has at some time or another been flying between New York and Los Angeles, and in their boredom looked out the window and noticed a country going by. 'Eureka!' they say into their airline pretzels, and yet another film involving sociopathic killers on the American Highway is born.

It seems any time characters are in middle America they are in a rush to get out. Once on the road there will be quirkiness, killing and/or bonding. Implicit in the conceit is that you have to be insane, stupid or both to live in the middle of portion of the USA.

Imagine if the number of films dedicated to this cluttered genre was proportional to its subject, I envisage highways choked with traffic jams of thrillkillers during 'spree high season'. When trusting local halfwits are not readily available, perhaps they resort to eliminating each other. Perhaps that is what has kept their populations in check all these years.

Among many of this genre suggested for but absent from this book are *Kalifornia*, *Clay Pigeons*, *Wild at Heart*, *Natural Born*

15

Killers and *True Romance*. So why aren't these films in the book? Because a genius, a poet and a painter on celluloid named Terrence Malick did it right the first time with *Badlands*.

In 1958, America was mesmerised by the killing spree of Charlie Starkweather and his girlfriend Caril-Ann Fugate, young Nebraskans who had internalised the cool attitudinising of antiheroes like James Dean and the romantic nihilism of movies such as *The Wild One* (1953) and *Rebel Without A Cause* (1955).

Martin Sheen and a very young Sissy Spacek portray Kit and Holly, a disaffected couple in a town out on the prairies where anything is better than nothing, and where a loser like Kit offers Holly more excitement than a scrutinising father (Warren Oates) and clarinet lessons can offer.

From the start, in her voice-over narration, Holly uses the unnatural and flowery diction of the gossip magazines she reads. She exaggerates their banal love and fumbling attempts at sex as the stuff of romances novels. When Holly escalates to killing, starting with her father, she rationalises his hair-trigger lethality with the same tabloid embellishment.

One of the themes that flow through Malick's films is the communal relationship humans have with the laws of nature, and that impulse has an implicit synchronicity with those laws; this concept goes a long way in explaining the characters' motivations.

Malick's visual sense has always been far more advanced than most of his contemporaries. He alternates carefully framed shots of intimacy in closed spaces, with sweeping vistas of earth and sky. There is a trance element to this film. It moves at such a slow pace, and is portrayed with such distance, that the narrative and the characters assume the same effect. Colour, physical dimension, perfectly nuanced music (Carl Orff) and low-key acting by the leads create something that's more a tone poem on America.

In the absence of any other perceived texture to their world, Kit and Holly create their own notion of it. In their world the prospect of something else, anything else, eclipses all the heartbreak of their situation. There is no comfort in the blandness of parental figures. In fact, to their thinking, all parental figures are themselves suspect. By Kit and Holly's estimation, if these authority figures had any sense, any ambition, any value at all, they wouldn't live in such a place. This allows Kit and Holly to turn their lethal self-loathing outward.

Both these kids substitute their own fantasies for any sense of order or responsibility. They feel no worth and even less power. In finding each other, they connect. They are able to actualise their hopes and find their sense of worth in becoming the other's ideal.

Kit is genuinely likeable and endearing – except for the whole 'shooting people' thing. This is typified when Kit shoots his friend with a shotgun, only to hold the screen door for him when he needs help inside the house.

▶▶

BARBARELLA: QUEEN OF THE GALAXY

Date:	1968
Director:	Roger Vadim
Writer(s):	Vittorio Bonicelli, Claude Brulé, Brian Degas, Jean-Claude Forest (also novel), Tudor Gates, Terry Southern, Roger Vadim, and Clement Biddle Wood
Runtime(s):	98 minutes
Country:	France, Italy
Language:	English

SEE BARBARELLA DO HER THING!

Ever wonder what it might look like if Gianni Versace had directed a Christmas pageant? Me neither, but it probably would have looked something like *Barbarella: Queen of the Galaxy*. It's a bizarre, futuristic take on Alice in Wonderland, full of beautiful people, quasi-surreal images and dated styles.

It has always fascinated me that you can tell as much about an era by how it chooses to envision the future as you can from the fashions and technology of its own time. *Barbarella* may be the antithesis of *2001: A Space Odyssey*, but they are both iconic artefacts of 1960s futurism. While *2001* was inspired by psychotropic and theological undertones of its era, *Barbarella* anticipates a year 40,000, wherein a retro craze for late-60s Las Vegas gouache will hold the entire universe in its thrall. Trends to look out for:

Weapons: OUT!
Fur lined interior rocket ships: IN!

Physical intercourse: OUT!
Pill-based pleasure simulation: IN!
Political correctness: So, so, sooo OUT!

The boa-clad president of Earth commissions sexy space
kitten Barbarella to save the galaxy to by locating a missing
scientist named Duran Duran. Barbarella crashes on a planet
and almost gets killed by children, meets a very hairy sail sled
driver (Ugo Tognazzi), gets laid, finds a handsome blind angel
(John Phillip Law), gets laid, finds a maze city, gets laid, finds her
way into the city, almost gets laid by the female 'Great Tyrant'
(Anita Pallenberg) who finds Barbarella 'pretty, pretty'. She
then finds herself in an underground guerilla movement, gets
(virtual pill-enhanced) laid by the movement 'leader' (David
Hemmings), finds the scientist (Milo O'Shea) and gets laid by
an organ; yes, I mean an actual organ, with pedals and keys.

Jane Fonda delivers all her lines with wide-eyed amazement,
like a sexually liberated version of Dorothy Gale in an erotic
Oz. As a sex object, Jane Fonda is at the absolute top of her
game in *Barbarella*. The film was made during a long-term love
affair between Fonda and director Roger Vadim, and it shows
in every frame. Many directors are in love with their lead, but
Vadim's camera does not linger over Fonda with unrequited
desire or fetish, but rather with an impassioned gaze of urgent
craving. Even the most hardened Vietnam veteran cannot deny
her allure. We can all agree Barbarella is 'pretty, pretty' indeed.

▶▶

BETTY BLUE /
37°2 LE MATIN

Date:	1986
Director:	Jean-Jacques Beineix
Writer(s):	Philippe Djian (novel), Jean-Jacques Beineix
Runtime(s):	120 minutes, 185 minutes (France, director's cut)
Country:	France
Language:	French

I HAD KNOWN BETTY FOR A WEEK.
WE MADE LOVE EVERY NIGHT.
THE FORECAST WAS FOR STORMS.

This is the film to embrace or avoid (depending on your predilection) if you have ever loved someone madly. If you have ever loved with intensity and against common sense, you will understand this film perfectly. It is one of the greatest portrayals I have ever seen of that dilemma. It is a very moving representation of love against reason, and the hope that sheer will can overcome mental illness.

Zorg (Jean-Hughes Anglade) is a shy, happy-go-lucky handyman and aspiring writer already in the throws of passion with Betty (Béatrice Dalle), a beautiful, free-spirited and probably manic-depressive young woman. Betty has trouble with authority and tends to get violent when provoked. Zorg finds her manic behaviour and cavalier demeanour refreshing as a counterbalance to his own tendency to withdraw.

After Zorg's boss makes too many unreasonable demands, Betty tosses everything out of their little chalet and torches it.

Apparently arson doesn't phase Zorg, so they set out in search of a better life. They take up a semi-nomadic existence together working in a restaurant for a time and then managing a piano shop. It turns out Zorg has written a hefty-sized book. Though Zorg is fairly apathetic about it, Betty believes passionately in Zorg's talent and expends tremendous energy attempting to get the book published. Every publisher's rejection contributes to the down-turn in Betty's mood. The deeper Zorg falls in love with Betty, the more he dismisses her unstable behaviour. Essentially, Zorg seems to expand to absorb Betty's extravagant character. Inevitably, Betty's insanity is triggered so dramatically as to leave no doubt to its presence. When Zorg's book finally achieves success, she is too damaged for the news to mean anything to her.

Sometimes life requires us to seek a complimentary opposite of ourselves, and not merely a reflection of our own temperament. The two leads have some of the greatest natural chemistry on film. This is made all the more remarkable that it is Béatrice Dalle's acting debut. She is the engine on this glorious ride.

The film is faithful to the sentimentality of Philippe Djian's original novel. It achieves some of the great emotional depth of a novel by cultivating 'mood' rather then the dull, numbing atmosphere one might expect from French cinema. *Betty Blue* prefers to focus on the 'manic' and not the 'depressive' side of Betty's condition and we feel the same energy around her that Zorg does. Employing some of the richest most colourful cinematography I have seen, and an excellent soundtrack, we are as entranced as he is. The film leads our emotions instead of manipulating them. It takes risks, never flinching from displays of raw emotion.

Much of the mystique surrounding *Betty Blue* comes from its eroticism. It is a very graphic film to be sure, but it is not gratuitous. There is a strong expression of mutual pleasure and commitment between the lovers and there are many other scenes outside bedrooms portraying their tenderness and companionship.

I appreciate the trust the film gives its audience. Anyone who is viewing this movie strictly for the sex would do better with lesser films. Likewise, anyone who cannot get past the sexuality, would probably miss the deeper themes altogether. Those of us who are left are grateful for the way it weaves emotional and physical intensity. Rather than one standing in for the other, this is the rare film that shows them as mutually sustaining.

If this description appeals to you, by all means view the director's cut. Likewise see it if you have seen and loved the general release version. The director's cut comes in at over 3 hours (185 minutes), so if you have only a neutral interest in the film, I would suggest the 120 minute general release version first.

▶▶

BLADE RUNNER

Date:	1982
Director:	Ridley Scott
Writer(s):	Philip K. Dick (novel), Hampton Fancher, David Webb Peoples and Roland Kibbee (voiceovers)
Runtime(s):	117 minutes (director's cut)
Country:	US
Language:	English

MAN HAS MADE HIS MATCH ... NOW IT'S HIS PROBLEM.

There are period films so influential they become the reference through which we imagine the era they portray. Seminal works like *Schindler's List* (1993) and *Barry Lyndon* (1975) define an archetypical conception for the eras they portray (the Holocaust and Georgian England respectively). The 1982 sci-fi classic *Blade Runner* was so influential in creating a richly textured portrayal of the coming techno/societal future, it's as if every cinematographer, art director and aspiring sci-fi writer since has accepted *Blade Runner*'s vision of 2019 as inevitable and irrefutable and merely reinterpret its construct.

Now an established classic, it is hard to believe that *Blade Runner* received very mixed reviews on its theatrical release in 1982. Based on the novel *Do Androids Dream of Electric Sheep?*, written by Philip K. Dick in 1968, it was the first big sci-fi film since *Star Wars* and its sequels. It was unjustly compared to these very different kinds of sci-fi movies, and derided for failing to fully recoup its initial $39 million budget.

Mixing action with calm, steady exposition, the film actually creates the gestalt of a noirish future through minute details. Every hint, every aspect of its world is both connected with our own and is also otherwise fully independent – with its own logic, technology, psychology, ethics and aesthetics. There is so much to take in visually, intellectually and emotionally and this film simply can't spoonfeed its meaning.

Synthetic people, called replicants, are created for and relegated to 'off-world' colonies. Occasionally, a few become upset with their subjugation and limited life spans. The film begins with a group of them having killed their human supervisors, and heading to Los Angeles to meet their maker, Tyrell (Joe Turkell), to request he extend their life spans past the allotted four years. This kind of incident is common enough to have sparked a specialist class of police called 'Blade Runners'. Rick Deckard (Harrison Ford), once a champion hunter of replicants, is called back from retirement to go take them down. Deckard is introduced to an 'Ultra Breed Replicant' named Rachel (Sean Young) by Tyrell. Deckard has a series of violent encounters with each renegade replicant while simultaneously falling in love with Rachel. Rachel, through artificial memory production, had not been aware of her replicant status and is now suffering an epic existential crisis. Rachel's dilemma complicates Deckard's sense of mission, and even forces him to second guess the authenticity of his own humanity. The trail of bloodshed leads inevitably to a showdown between Deckard and 'Alpha Replicant' Roy Batty (Rutger Hauer) that ends more on a note of philosophical closure than traditional action climax.

The Vangelis soundtrack is incredible. It adds beautifully to the immensity of the visuals, while never eclipsing the emotional undercurrents. The scene-stealer of *Blade Runner* may be the incredible set design and photography, but what really lifts this movie are the philosophical undertones: What is the essence of being human? Is life's value measured by longevity or by how time is spent? And what responsibility does man have when he creates life? It's the old *Frankenstein* question posed on the cusp of a new millennium in which it may soon become a real issue of bioethics.

There is a real debate over whether the director's cut or the original American theatrical release is superior. The original release tends to be derided for its optimistic ending and the use of voiceover narration by Harrison Ford. The director's cut has a more abrupt and ambiguous ending, excises the narration and includes the hyper-symbolic 'Unicorn Scene'. While most auteur viewers prefer the director's cut, I have to admit I miss the narration from the original release. As well as adding exposition on 2019 society, and generally being well written, the voiceover is a key element in the overall 'futuristic noir' the film seeks to create. The truth is both cuts have strengths and weaknesses and as *Blade Runner* deserves more than one viewing, you might be best served to see both cuts and decide for yourself.

Blade Runner holds up very well, even 20 years after its release. But with its enduring influence on art direction in film, television, video games and music videos, how could it not?

▶▶

BLUE VELVET

Date:	1986
Director:	David Lynch
Writer(s):	David Lynch
Runtime(s):	120 minutes
Country:	US
Language:	English

IT'S A STRANGE WORLD.

Blue Velvet received only one 1986 Oscar nomination, for Best
Director. I had always found the distinction between Best
Director and Best Picture Academy Awards absurd. Wouldn't
the best work in directing necessarily create the best picture?
Blue Velvet is the picture that illustrated to me the purpose
behind separate categories. This film is most distinct not for its
story or performances, but the stylistic imprint of it's director.
It's an interesting composite of performances, imagery and
a musical score by Badalamenti that not only underpins the
eeriness, but occasionally even leads it. The film is thick with
mood.

As far as plot, it's not entirely complicated. Jeffrey Beaumont
(Kyle MacLachlan) discovers a severed ear in a patch of grass
and endeavours to find out whose it is and how it got there.
That's pretty much it.

Blue Velvet is more a play of ideas than a straightforward,
plot-driven film. It's part traditional film noir mystery, part
satire of small-town life, with a strong thread of perverse
eroticism: a commentary on the dark underbelly of a seemingly
benign society.

26

David Lynch establishes a mood of naive innocence and virtue, then abruptly scrapes it away to reveal the dark sickness lurking beneath. It is a forte he displays in subsequent works – *Twin Peaks* (1990), *Wild at Heart* (1990), *Lost Highway* (1997) and *Mulholland Drive* (2001) – but established here. Tranquillity is a state most vigorously defended by not looking too closely beneath. Just as in the opening of the movie, when the perfect lawn in the perfect town is revealed to be infested with insects, the film unfolds to reveal the depth of evil in the person of one Frank Booth (Dennis Hopper).

Jeffrey's mother (Priscilla Pointer) warns him to avoid 'Lincoln Street'. Every town in America has its own Lincoln Street, a locus of disapproval, a 'bad area', concentrated and distinct from more desirable neighbourhoods. As evidenced by apartment buildings, which are transient and communitarian, the Lincoln Streets of America are peopled by those not living a settled life. It is simpler to ascribe failure to these people than choice, because in assuming failure, one assumes they at least share the mainstream value system even if they have been unsuccessful. A more threatening notion is that one chooses not to participate in polite company. This element would be, by the definition of polite company, unbalanced. Just as when Frank Booth declares, 'Heineken? Fuck that shit! Pabst Blue Ribbon!' (It's lowrent American beer.)

Blue Velvet was an interesting statement in the middle of the Reagan era. It was a time when sustaining the illusion of the settled orderly life was more important than actually creating it. This illusion had to be imposed like a flat set from another era, which is how the sets in *Blue Velvet* appear. There is an anachronistic blend of elements in Lynch's world and it feels intentional. The sets with their shabby furnishings and liver-coloured decor are never meant to look real. Continuity would give too much form to the film, what is projected instead is understated chaos; an anxiety that all is not right. The tension pays off when it explodes. And oh how it explodes.

The 'heroine' Dorothy Vallens (Isabella Rossellini) is iconic. Whether it is fair to Isabella Rossellini or not, her resemblance to her mother Ingrid Bergman is striking. Every shot of Rossellini projects classic Hollywood elegance. This grace is literally brutalised and degraded by Booth. Further unsettling is that Dorothy, who appears to be the paragon of the feminine ideal, does not in fact want to be saved. Sadism fascinates her. Her willingness to participate with Booth undermines the relationship between, as well as the very definitions of, a traditional 'villain' and an unwilling 'victim'.

Each time I re-examine *Blue Velvet*, I find it a richer and more challenging experience. It is a piece more interested in setting off chords within the viewer than offering solutions. A film one does not watch once, but rather with which one develops a relationship over time.

▶▶

THE BLUES BROTHERS

Date:	1980
Director:	John Landis
Writer(s):	Dan Aykroyd and John Landis
Runtime(s):	133 minutes, 148 minutes
	(USA, extended version)
Country:	USA
Language:	English

THEY'LL NEVER GET CAUGHT.
THEY'RE ON A MISSION FROM GOD.

They're 'on a Mission from G-ahhd!' Not 'God', let alone the high-English, biblical epic 'GAUGHD', but pure Chicago Ethnic-Catholic 'G-ahhd'. *The Blues Brothers* follows siblings Elwood Blues (Dan Aykroyd) and fresh-out-of-prison 'Joliet' Jake Blues (John Belushi) as they try to re-unite their blues combo. They do this in order to raise $5,000 to save the orphanage in which they grew up.

Its loose plot creates a chain of vignettes and musical numbers that are at once over-the-top and strangely authentic to the blues experience. It is a loving homage to blues music. The musical cameos – from John Lee Hooker, Aretha Franklin, James Brown and Ray Charles – are fantastic. Cab Calloway does a rendition of 'Minnie Moocher' that is a tribute to his own showmanship.

But it is also a very funny representation of the below-the-margin existence that both inspires the blues and is the domain of those who endeavour to do it for a living: bad gigs, woman problems, poverty and, of course, Nazis.

The Blues Brothers features the strangest amalgam of enemies in cinema history: the Illinois State Police, the Chicago Police, the National Guard, a country and western band, a jilted hairdresser and the Illinois Nazi Party. John Landis was deft enough to use the loose plot structure as a license to throw a bunch of disparate characters into motion. In lesser hands this would have meant chaos. But each character is driven by such white-hot contempt for the brothers that they are woven together to a single magnificent conclusion.

One can tell this is a fondly conceived film. 'The Blues Brothers' first appeared on *Saturday Night Live*. Belushi and Aykroyd created the characters strictly as a pre-broadcast warm-up act (as much for their own performance energy as for the studio audience). It is a blend of broad and subtle comedy. There are literally thousands of car wrecks countered with some of the coolest understated reactions ever seen on film. The sublime moments are genius: my brothers and I never to fail to laugh at the strange qualification and specificity to the line, 'I hate Illinois Nazis.'

This film is also in love with Chicago, and Chicago with it. So personal is my relationship to the film as a Chicagoan, I was amazed to discover the passionate following it has worldwide, particularly in the UK. It has the same local identification that Edinburgh must have with *Trainspotting* (1996). In being so authentically local, its sincerity registers universally.

It's such a glorious mix of hilarious situations, quotable lines and superb characters. Dan Aykroyd has yet to find a roll to eclipse our memory of Elwood. And great performances abound in small parts from other actors: Carrie Fisher ('waiting in celibacy!'), Charles Napier ('we're the Good Ole Boys'), Kathleen Freeman (a nun known as 'the penguin'), John Candy ('Orange whip? Orange whip? Three orange whips?'),

Henry Gibson ('and he's a Catho-lic') and Ray Charles ('I hate to see a boy that young go bad'). Also look for cameos by two famous directors: Frank Oz ('soiled') and Steven Spielberg (the Cook County Clerk) in one of the few parts where he doesn't play himself.

It goes without saying that John Belushi died way too young. *The Blues Brothers* remains a testament to what he was capable of doing, and a standard for all musicals and comedies when pure joy, energy and commitment are permitted to exceed the boundaries of 'formula'.

▸▸

Brazil

Date:	1985
Director:	Terry Gilliam
Writer(s):	Terry Gilliam, Charles McKeown and Tom Stoppard
Runtime(s):	131 minutes, 142 minutes (USA, director's cut)
Country:	UK
Language:	English

IT'S ONLY A STATE OF MIND.

When Kafka wrote *The Trial*, he set it out of any specific point in history, making it contemporary to all time. Whereas in 1948, when George Orwell wrote *1984*, it had a necessarily futuristic element to it. When Terry Gilliam fused both these stories into his intellectually loaded and visually remarkable masterpiece, *Brazil*, one of the many ingenious aspects lay in his recognising that he was making both a contemporary film and a film out-of-time. He therefore created his own 'meta-reality'.

In *Brazil*, a generic Western society has become a bureaucratic web. The simplest exchange requires mountains of paperwork and strict adherence to procedures has replaced anyone's ability to critically think about the banality and brutality around them. Sam Lowry (Jonathan Pryce) is an anonymous functionary in a bland government ministry, 'Information Management'. Much to the consternation of his upper class mother, Sam has repeatedly turned down promotions to the more prestigious ministry of 'Information Retrieval'. Sam prefers to live happily and quietly as a cog in the giant machine. When Sam sleeps, however, he flies through beautiful blue skies toward the woman of his dreams.

One day a bug (literally) in the system creates a whirlwind of mistakes. A request has been made for the detention of Archibald 'Harry' Tuttle (Robert De Niro), a vigilante freedom fighter/air-conditioner repairman who doesn't play by Central Services' (the government's physical plant) rules. Unfortunately a bug falls into a typewriter while the request is processed, mistakenly creating a report for 'Buttle', a low-key, poor family man. The error results in the innocent man's arrest and eventual death.

Sam attempts to 'correct' this 'oversight' by the ministry by delivering an 'arrest refund cheque' to Buttle's widow. There, he meets Jill Layton (Kim Greist), who is (again, literally) the girl of his dreams. Motivated by concern for her neighbour, Jill has been enquiring about Buttle's disappearance. Upon recognising Jill from his dreams, Sam eagerly accepts the promotion he has been turning down in order to more authoritatively investigate the Buttle case, and thereby make himself more attractive to Jill.

The line between his dreams and reality blur ever further as he goes deeper and deeper into the government machine to find out who Jill is. Meanwhile, his air-conditioner breaks and his call to Central Services is intercepted by none other than Tuttle. When Central Services finally does respond, the two repairmen, Spoor and Charlie (Bob Hoskins and Nigel Planer) are suspicious, and they vengefully take over Lowry's apartment for 'repair reasons'.

Eventually, Sam does win Jill's heart. Fearing Jill will be wanted for sedition because of her enquiries, he endeavours to erase her identity from the central computer system.

Terry Gilliam seems to have spared no expense in making sure every visual element of the world adds up to a cohesive whole. It is a world rendered realistically enough to feel feasible, and yet surrealistically enough to leave an unforgettable impression on you. Gilliam's stroke of genius was to meld these elements so thoroughly with a fantasy world that it's hard to discern where one ends and the other starts.

By setting *Brazil* 'somewhere in the twentieth century', he employs an odd use of retro-design, taking elements from the past 80 years and fusing them into one world. The upper-class social circle has a 1920s feel to it. This makes it seem both cloistered from the squalor and menace of its surrounding world, and imbues its excesses with the imminent doom of that era

The film also fits many genres: comedy, drama, sci-fi, social critique, etc. You can try to explain the plot to people in a one-line summary: a man looks for his dream woman and is crushed by the state. This is too simple for a film so rich in subplots and thematic allusions, but this through-line allows something upon which all the other aspects can be hung without losing focus. Thus many sub-textual images can flourish: in one scene, a man is buying 'clean air' from a vending machine along the street; the sides of the highways are walls of billboards, which hide the barren environment beyond; a group of people carry a banner that announces 'Consumers for Christ' in a store decorated for the holidays as a small child tells Santa she wants a credit card for Christmas.

Brazil is less about the overt totalitarianism of *1984*, and more about submission to a slower, more polite death. There are no choices in this society. One can neither fail nor succeed. Sam seems as rebellious as one is able to be, by continuing to turn down promotions. The promotion itself is no reflection on Sam's abilities (which are displayed): instead his destiny is determined by nepotism. In lieu of any other effective rebellion, Sam rebels against success.

This is definitely a big screen film, meant to be viewed from beginning to end without interruption. The sheer momentum of the social critique and humour end up hitting you like a train by the film's end, an experience which simply can't be replicated when viewed with the visual limitations and concentration interferences of watching TV at home. One needs to focus on the mood of oppressive reality-unreality and Sam's reaction to it. This mood holds up throughout the film and is the film's greatest gift.

▶▶

CARNIVAL OF SOULS

Date:	1962
Director:	Herk Harvey
Writer(s):	John Clifford
Runtime:	78 minutes, 84 minutes (USA, director's cut)
Country:	US
Language:	English

IS THERE DEATH AFTER LIFE?

Hailed as a low budget unintentional horror masterpiece, *Carnival of Souls* has become the standard for the late 50s, early 60s genre of American horror. Yet, conversely, it also seems to transcend the category entirely. Its deliberate pacing and unorthodox composition elements honestly seem more attuned to the sensibilities of contemporary, French new-wave cinema than its counterparts in American drive-in fare. Whether through its limited resources, or by conscious choice, *Carnival of Souls* ends up illustrating truth in the auteur's axiom 'less is more'.

In 1962, industrial film director Herk Harvey decided to make a horror film. He had previously made about 40 films for school and industry with such titles as: *What About School Spirit?* (1958), *Caring for Your Toys* (1954), *Street Safety Is Your Problem* (1952) and *Your Junior High Days* (1961). He enlisted the help of fellow Kansans John Clifford (screenplay) and Maurice Prather (cinematographer) to help him, and they recruited local talent to act in the film. The lead character, Mary Henry (Candace Hilligoss), only appeared in one other film.

The film opens with Mary Henry involved in a drag race

in rural Kansas that results in her car driving off of a bridge into a river. She manages to walk away from the accident, but afterwards is haunted by a ghoulish-looking man. She ends up getting a job as an organist at a church in Salt Lake City where the apparition still appears. She also feels compelled to visit an old, abandoned carnival.

The technical inadequacies add to the surreal, dream-like atmosphere of the film. It is in direct opposition to the Ed Wood 'so bad it's good' school of camp cinema. This film knows its limitations and acts brilliantly with what is possible (rather than reaching beyond its scope). In other words, a director with more options might not choose to focus so effectively on the elements that were available to Harvey. Watch how he lights a Utah plain. He found sets that could be had for next-to-nothing. See how he creates a Midwestern Hades with simple lighting and make-up. The low-budget make-up is also very effective, giving the zombies a surreal, *Three Penny Opera* effect that complements the tone. He then takes advantage of (and perhaps encouraged) the stiffness of amateur actors, creating a stilted and distant reality.

He also utilises what I consider one of the most compelling effects in a movie: silence. Those scenes when the sound goes out are just brilliantly filmed, and producing that effect probably actually saved them money. I love the way there is only gentle organ music throughout, and then the sound of wind blowing under the pier, near the end of the film. The heavy, clunking footsteps that prevail on the soundtrack sound death-like, exaggerated and very, very unreal.

After making this film, Herk Harvey and John Clifford continued working for the same industrial film company as if nothing had happened. Over the years the movie started fading away from peoples' memories until the advent of VHS tapes. The movie was a popular rental and low-budget television staple (particularly in Australia). It developed a cult following which prompted Candace Hilligoss to contact an ageing Herk Harvey to try and make a sequel or remake.

The 1998 remake is to be avoided. But if you've seen *The Sixth Sense* you'll see that it also owes a debt to *Carnival of Souls*.

▶▶

A Clockwork Orange

Date:	1971
Director:	Stanley Kubrick
Writer(s):	Anthony Burgess (novel), Stanley Kubrick
Runtime(s):	137 minutes
Country:	UK
Language:	English

BEING THE ADVENTURES OF A YOUNG MAN
WHOSE PRINCIPAL INTERESTS ARE
RAPE, ULTRA-VIOLENCE AND
BEETHOVEN.

Alex DeLarge (Malcolm McDowell) is the leader of a quartet of 'droogs' in an unspecified English city in the near future. They spend their nights raping, brawling, attacking helpless drunks and breaking into houses.

Fissures develop in the group when two of the four members, Dim (Warren Clarke) and Georgie (James Marcus), express an unwillingness to continue blindly following Alex's lead. Alex's response is to slash both of them. They bide their time and nurse their wounds until the opportunity arises to set Alex up. They strike at the scene of a botched burglary/murder, knocking him senseless and leaving him for the police. He is tried, convicted and sentenced to 14 years in prison.

Alex becomes a model prisoner, upon whom the Minister of the Interior, anxious to reduce the prison population, allows brainwashing experiments to be conducted. He is sent to the Ludovico centre where he is forced to watch footage of brutal beatings, rape and Nazi marches all the while with good-old

Ludwig van Beethoven's *Ninth Symphony* playing in the background. Doctors pump Alex full of nausea-producing drugs, developing a negative Pavlovian response to immoral and illegal activities. As the treatment slowly works, Alex screams in agony as he begins to feel sick at the sight of violence.

Alex comes out of the Ludovico Centre a changed man. Or is he?

The film is a stylistic masterpiece. The environment of *Clockwork* is very much an early-70s British dystopia: multistory flats with space-age tunnels, awash in litter, infesting the edges of the green belt. Alex and his droogs use much of Burgess' made-up slang language, Nadsat. The group is a mishmash of British subcultural styles – a bit of teddy boy, part boot boy, even part Mod. They swagger in bowler hats and speak with prole accents. They intersect with Britain at the time of the film's production – one of labour disputes and mainland bombings – yet there is enough of a futuristic tone (albeit a bleak one) to also make Alex and company harbingers of a world to come.

In the opening sequence with the droogs, the system is revealed to be impotent – ineffectual in all its deliberation and justifications. In its failure to assert any discernable purpose, the rule of nature rises unchallenged. Visceral power is the only valued force. Such is Alex's attraction to Beethoven – it is not a reflection of high taste, rather a natural attraction to genius, power and force.

The theme of modified behaviour versus actual contrition is a strong one. Kubrick achieves this nicely by degenerating Alex to a broken animal. Alex is not reformed, merely subdued, bereft of human dignity. It seems that a culture that resorts to such measures has no moral imperative to govern. When an emasculated Alex encounters his former victims, each of them acts vengefully toward the helpless Alex. In a turn of events, Alex encounters a homeless victim, his former droogs who have since become constables and finally an intellectual openly opposed to behaviour modification. Each of his victims loses a bit of humanity in their vengeance. It seems an indictment of revenge punishment as it does behaviour modification. The only true change comes from the greatest gift of conscious beings: free will.

In 1971, *A Clockwork Orange* won two awards from the New York Film Critic's Circle: Best Picture and Best Director. The Academy recognised the picture with four Oscar nominations, including Best Picture, Best Director and Best Screenplay. The British Academy followed suit, topping the American total with six. And the public-friendly Golden Globes accorded *A Clockwork Orange* a trio of nominations – one for the film, one for the director, and one for Malcolm McDowell as Best Actor.

In 1974 Stanley Kubrick withdrew *A Clockwork Orange* from distribution in Britain. He had felt threatened and undermined by the film's reception: people called it obscene and accused it of glorifying violence. Kubrick was not wrong to feel threatened – the film was hated in a very personal way, and threats were made against him – and in time claims of 'copycat' violence would be used to damn the film even further. For 28 years he refused to re-release it. Following Kubrick's death, UK distributors agreed the film could be screened again. I suppose the irony of suppressing a film that explores the morality of mind control became too blatant even for them.

▶▶

DAWN OF THE DEAD

Date:	1978
Director:	George A. Romero
Writer(s):	George A. Romero, Dario Argento (uncredited)
Runtime(s):	126 minutes, 156 minutes (Germany, complete version), 117 minutes (Italy, Dario Argento's European/Italian cut), 139 minutes (USA, director's cut)
Country:	USA, Italy
Language:	English

... WHEN THERE'S NO MORE ROOM IN HELL, THE DEAD WILL WALK THE EARTH.

George Romero's *Night of the Living Dead* (1968) is a low-budget classic, there is no disputing that. His second zombie feature *Dawn of the Dead*, however, is a bigger and more audacious film. Not exactly a sequel, *Dawn of the Dead* explores parallel themes with an expanded budget. I chose it over the first because one imagines that this is the film Romero wanted to make in the first place. And I for one am glad he did. It builds on the spirit and ideas of the original while establishing an identity of its own.

The film has all the elements crucial to effective storytelling: great atmosphere, sympathetic characters and urgent pacing. It is this delicate crafting that allows some films to transcend mere horror. The characters ask the questions we would ask and take the steps we would take, and without being predictable it manages to always choose the most sensible path.

As civil society breaks down amid the worldwide rise of the living dead, SWAT team members Peter Washington (Ken

Foree) and Roger Demarco (Scott H. Reiniger), and traffic reporters Stephen Andrews (David Emge) and Francine Parker (Gaylen Ross), escape in a helicopter. They come across a deserted suburban Philadelphia shopping mall and break in through the roof.

After fighting the zombies they manage to secure the mall and stock up on supplies, until they find themselves besieged by a motorcycle gang, who would rather kill them in order to loot the mall than band together against the zombies.

Setting the standoff in a shopping mall is simply a brilliant choice. It creates apocalyptic menace in a usually benign setting; the stores give the characters a variety of resources for defending themselves and, not least, it delivers an intentional and hilarious social comment. When is the last time you heard anyone debate the political subtext of an American film, let alone a horror film? Given the variety of interpretations, the obvious dichotomy between a barricaded few who are stocked and well armed and those who are a horde of the poor and hungry makes for a brutal conflict.

Horror films in which everybody can become the monster always seem to have higher stakes. It is a fate worse than death; it is denigration and the loss of one's will. It's hard not to have sympathy for the zombies. Their only fault is to be resurrected and wander in blind craving. The humans meanwhile operate out of choice and display remarkable greed. The moral heart of the film, for me, is best represented by an old priest who surprises two of the characters in a tenement basement: 'When the dead walk, we must stop the killing, or we lose the war.'

Don't get me wrong in praising the subtext; the film is also gloriously, delightfully excessive. Horror make-up and special effects master Tom Savini splatters his mark all over this one. The film is actually so violent and gruesome that it was released unrated in the United States for fear of being slapped with an X Rating. Yet other moments are downright sublime. At one point Peter and Stephen respectfully walk around the ropes used for queuing in a completely abandoned bank. In another instance, one of the bikers gets his intestines torn out by a zombie because he stops to get his blood pressure checked.

Dawn of the Dead was a collaboration made in 'horror heaven'. Italian horror maestro Dario Argento helped secure funding for the film, in exchange for the right to oversee the international cut of the film. Dario Argento also served as an uncredited writer and helped with the score using his band The Goblins. But ultimately it is George Romero's direction that makes this film a classic.

▶▶

THE DAY THE CLOWN CRIED

Date:	1972
Director:	Jerry Lewis
Writer(s):	Charles Denton, Jerry Lewis, Joan O'Brien
Runtime(s):	(not applicable)
Country:	US, Sweden
Language:	English

DEAR GOD WHY?

What thread connects the varying projects elevated to 'cult film' status? There is no single definition to be sure, but as you browse this book you will appreciate the recurrence of exaggerated fascination developed by viewers for a specific film. At times this enormous interest is inversely proportional to the actual size of the audience. In other words: small audience plus huge fascination equals 'cult film'. This logic necessitates including a film that has managed to become a true Hollywood legend and yet has been seen by less than 20 people.

The film is the notorious *The Day the Clown Cried* based on a story about a dislikeable, unsuccessful (and gentile) German circus clown named Karl Schmidt who was sent to Auschwitz for satirising Hitler and was subsequently used by his Nazi captors to lead unsuspecting Jewish children into the gas chamber. Yes, someone wrote it. Someone else read it and actually said, 'Yes, let's do it!' Someone financed it and someone even shot it.

Sometime around 1972, director, star and egomaniac Jerry Lewis embarked on this bizarre and arguably questionable film project. Through a series of financial missteps, personal conflicts and legal complications, the film was never released. The production's irregularities left the question of rights in a snarl: claiming that it is owed more than $600,000, the studio in Stockholm has held on to the negative; the screenwriters own the copyright and won't allow its completion. In fact, only a rough cut was ever completed and that cut remains vigorously protected.

And so *The Day the Clown Cried* has become a source of unending rumour, an embodiment of wrong-headed egotism, a five-word joke and a holy grail for collectors of rare film clips. Countless people have been left to speculate, 'Could it possibly be as bad as it sounds?' The answer, as much as has been made available to the general public, is 'yes'. Comedian and writer Harry Shearer actually viewed a cut of the film in 1979 and had this to say: 'This movie is so drastically wrong, its pathos and its comedy are so wildly misplaced, that you could not, in your fantasy of what it might be like, improve on what it really is. Oh My God! – that's all you can say.'

The script had actually been written ten years earlier by Joan O'Brien, a former PR woman, and Charles Denton, a TV critic for the *Los Angeles Examiner*. *The Day the Clown Cried* was supposed to be Lewis' first serious film as both director and star: 'a turning point in the career of one of the most unusual performers in history', according to the movie's press kit, adding that Lewis is 'a 20th Century … phenomenon like atomic energy, moonshot, heart transplants, and hippies …' Apparently he believed his own press to the point of rewriting the script, changing the protagonist's name from Karl Schmidt to the more distinctive – and more 'Jerry-Lewis-movie'-like – Helmut Doork.

The original story was supposedly a tale of horror, conceit and, finally, enlightenment and self-sacrifice. Jerry had turned it into a sentimental, Chaplinesque representation of his own confused sense of himself, his art, his charity work and his persecution at the hands of critics. Furthermore, he had used the clown theme as an occasion to work into the film some of the silent routines he had been performing in Europe.

The Lewis penned shooting script – some 164 pages – has been circulating on the Internet ever since *Film Threat* magazine procured and disseminated a copy. Not only is the writing incoherent and the technical cues baffling (the script specifically notes when things should be 'played for laughs'), flourishes of vanity and discontinuity hindered the actual shooting. According to those who have seen it, Lewis the celebrity trounced Lewis the director on a number of points. He literally has slicked back hair throughout. In one scene Jerry is lying in his bunk wearing a pair of brand new shoes after theoretically having been in a concentration camp for four or five years.

The Day the Clown Cried is probably lost for ever. Lewis has a copy of the rough cut on videotape. He reportedly keeps it in his office, in a Louis Vuitton briefcase (because anything gauche would not suit this script). Over the years, he has screened it – or pieces of it – for a number of colleagues and at least one journalist. But there is hope for the rest of us. 'One way or another, I'll get it done,' Jerry Lewis vows in his autobiography. 'The picture must be seen, and if by no one else, at least by every kid in the world who's only heard there was such a thing as the Holocaust.'

▶▶

DONNIE DARKO

Date:	2001
Director:	Richard Kelly
Writer(s):	Richard Kelly
Runtime(s):	113 minutes
Country:	US
Language:	English

DARK, DARKEST, DARKO.

Donnie Darko is the most recent film to qualify for this book, and there is no doubt that it has already garnered a cult following. For over two years it has enjoyed an uninterrupted run in New York City, every Friday and Saturday at midnight at the Pioneer Theater. Even if the film fades from popular consciousness, it still may serve the purposes of this book by illustrating some of the elements of cult cinema and how self-awareness affects whether an audience embraces a film.

If pressed to give rules regarding cult films, I have imagined there would be only one rule; that one may not set out to purposely make a cult film. It's like giving yourself a nickname – there is simply no way to do it. However, *Donnie Darko* seems to be a film constructed from a recipe of cult cinema elements. It self-consciously endeavours to be a cult film, and in so doing makes no small effort in informing viewers that they should agree. If the aforementioned rule were true, this would disqualify *Donnie Darko*. Yet it has had a resonant effect on a devoted audience in a very brief time. And so I have learned that the only rule to cult films is that there truly are no fixed rules.

It is a very earnest first effort from director Richard Kelly. It does well with visual effects on a small budget and has an interesting twist on the trend of non-linear storytelling. But like many debut features, it is ambitious in its scope, yet leaves very little ambiguity in how it hopes we interpret the elements presented. The film seems to italicise every point it makes. Whether due to its fondness for its own cleverness, a lack of trust by the filmmakers for their audience or a mixture of both, the film is unbelievably self-referential. It's almost algebraic in its effort to concisely tie together every bit of foreshadowing.

Donnie (Jake Gyllenhaal) is a middle class, smart but depressed and slightly sullen American teen who takes medication for schizophrenia. Donnie frequently wanders off in the middle of the night in a hallucinatory daze. A recurring symptom of his delusion involves a demonic rabbit who challenges Donnie with existential questions, leads him to and occasionally persuades the boy to commit acts of vandalism.

During one such night, Donnie is lured from his bed by these night terrors. After awakening on a golf course, Donnie comes home to find an engine has mysteriously fallen off a jet liner and crashed into his family's home. The rest of the family is unharmed and the home is spared except for Donnie's room which has been all but crushed. The delusions have saved Donnie's life, and the rest of the film weaves connections between fate, sanity and the time–space continuum.

Jake is very believable as Donnie. Considering this is a sci-fi film, it succeeds remarkably well as a character study, a rumination on mental illness and how family relationships are affected. I was impressed with how sympathetically Donnie's parents (Holmes Osborne and Mary McDonnell) are portrayed. They are concerned about Donnie's condition, but reluctant to fixate on it lest they make it worse. They seem to cope with it, attempting not to deny Donnie's condition so much as sustaining normalcy while waiting for medication to do what it can. Likewise, Donnie's sister Elizabeth (played by Jake's real-life sister Maggie Gyllenhaal) affects a wise and patient affection for her brother.

There are a lot of concepts vying for attention here: time travel, death, life, religion, teen angst, parents living vicariously through their children, parents misunderstanding their children and first love.

It's 1988. Lest we forget its 1988, there are frequent references to the US presidential election and extended sequences set to 1988 appropriate alterna-rock (Echo and the Bunnymen, The Church, Tears for Fears, etc). Plus the always precious pop culture references, including smurf sex theory and Hungry Hungry Hippos inspired existential disappointment.

If the pacing and plotline have failed to establish a sense of foreboding, not to worry; story cards appear frequently to describe the amount of days left to a mysterious occurrence. Just in case the trans-dimensional science is not clear enough for us, the film invokes a science teacher played by Noah Wyle to postulate on every metaphysical principle.

Producer Drew Barrymore miscasts herself as a darkly earnest and intellectually sympathetic English teacher who becomes a victim of her own combination of enlightened tolerance and strong convictions. A lively debate over a Graham Greene short story is introduced, both to emphasise concurrent themes at work in *Donnie Darko* and to confirm the rather tired cliché that all conservatives have southern accents, are dimwitted and operate out of repressed desire for the very things they condemn. The embodiment of which is a slightly out-of-place subplot involving a Dianetics-meets-pentacostal motivational speaker portrayed by Patrick Swayze.

Limitations aside, the film has generated great affection among those who have seen it, perhaps because it was a labour of love for those involved. It is undeniably an ambitious film, its quality far beyond the limitations of its shoe-string budget. Perhaps because the film was initially mis-marketed as a horror film (which it is not), it may have gained momentum as a kind of 'sleeper', gaining positive word-of-mouth buzz. It definitely rises above and defies the expectations created by the trailer.

▶▶

▶ # DOWN BY LAW

Date:	1986
Director:	Jim Jarmusch
Writer(s):	Jim Jarmusch
Runtime(s):	107 minutes
Country:	US, West Germany
Language:	English

IT'S NOT WHERE YOU START –
IT'S WHERE YOU START AGAIN.

Jim Jarmusch is one of the filmmakers whose entire body of work – *Stranger than Paradise* (1983), *Down by Law* (1986), *Mystery Train* (1989), *Night on Earth* (1991), *Dead Man* (1995) and *Ghost Dog: The Way of the Samurai* (1999) – has garnered a cult following. There is a distinctive 'Jarmusch style' running through his films, most evident in his pacing. He relishes taking his time, indicating his characters with odd, seemingly incidental details that say as much as any heavy exposition.

It is often difficult to choose a single film when there is a cult around the director's body of work. Comparable in many ways to another contemporary American cult director, Hal Hartley, each Jarmusch film is a step in the artist's evolution. The scope, budgets and themes may expand with each picture, but an unmistakable style is imprinted on all. All his signature flourishes are in evidence in Jarmush's second feature *Down by Law*. A low-budget, black-and-white cult favourite from 1986, *Down by Law* establishes a kind of tight continuity because of its limited resources.

Jack (John Lurie), a big-talking small-timer and ineffectual pimp, Zack (Tom Waits), an itinerant disk jockey with a mane of messy hair and pointy-toed shoes, and Roberto 'Bob' (Roberto Benigni) end up in the same Louisiana jail cell. Jack and Zack are framed for child prostitution and murder respectively. Bob, an Italian who speaks very little English, is locked up because he killed a man with a poolball. Jack thinks he has a voodoo curse on him; Zack merely drove a dead body to another town for a few dollars. And while Bob comes across as the most innocent of the group, he is ironically is the only one who is actually guilty.

Jack and Zack may hate each other. But hate is nothing compared to the emotions they feel for the Italian, who commits the unpardonable sin of being constantly cheerful. Bob writes down American figures of speech and repeats them in his exaggerated accent. When he is introduced to the expression, 'You scream. I scream. We all scream for ice cream,' he repeats it from his notepad and soon incites the prison to riot chanting: 'You scream! I scream. We ALL scream for ice cream!'

It is telling that the three end up escaping not from jail's harshness but its mind-numbing boredom. I love that the prison break, which would be the crux of most films, is never shown or diagrammed. It is merely discussed, and in the next shot the three are outside and on the l am. Likewise there is no courtroom sentencing, nor an explanation of why Zack and Jack were set up. These plot points are inconsequential as this is a relationship film.

All Jarmusch films feature people whose mutual dependency is not deterred by their inability to understand one another. He uses a multitude of devices including language barriers, race, gender, musical preferences, class, personal morality and family to illustrate this. There may be animosity about the effort required to connect with one another: Ellen Barkin has a wonderful cameo as Zack's girlfriend, whose tantrum culminates in his possessions being thrown into the street. Again it is not the disdain between characters so much as the frustration in their not connecting that drives her over the edge.

There are good performances in this film. Tom Waits is not simply a talented musician dabbling in acting; he is a vessel of soulful heartache that can convey sympathy in any medium he chooses (one need only to have seen him shine as strongly as co-stars Streep and Nicholson in *Ironweed* to know this). But this film is absolutely carried by Roberto Benigni. He lights up the screen so effortlessly and infectiously that it is no wonder he affects those around him as strongly as he does. He is a genius of charisma, and the scenes with his real-life wife Nicoletta Braschi foretell and perhaps even eclipse their charming chemistry in *La Vita E Bella* (Life is Beautiful).

Down by Law works so well due to timing. You can't rush this film. Every gesture is significant in meaning and consequence. It takes its time expressing the solitude of its characters, but never broods. The characters seem to inadvertently provoke rather than react, creating the necessary pretext for the endearingly awkward connections. Enjoy.

▶▶

DR. STRANGELOVE OR: HOW I LEARNED TO STOP WORRYING AND LOVE THE BOMB

Date:	1964
Director:	Stanley Kubrick
Writer(s):	Terry Southern, Stanley Kubrick, Peter George (III) (novel)
Runtime(s):	93 minutes
Country:	UK
Language:	English, Russian

THE HOT-LINE SUSPENSE COMEDY.

The sheer audacity of attempting a dark comedy about nuclear annihilation at the height of the Cold War and only months after the assassination of President John Kennedy, would have assured Stanley Kubrick cult filmmaker status.

When US General Jack D. Ripper (Sterling Hayden) orders wing attack plan R into operation he sets planes on an irreversible bombing run into Russia. Powerless to stop them without the relevant three letter access code, the US President (Peter Sellars) and his advisors plan to warn Russia as best they can to prevent as many of the planes reaching their targets as possible. However, when the Russian Ambassador (Peter Bull) warns of the doomsday machine – a machine that will destroy all life on earth in response to a nuclear attack – things look bleak.

Well shot, well written and well acted, it is a masterpiece of filmmaking. Kubrick embraced black and white when filmmakers began embracing it as an artistic choice. Camera composition and the use of light make every frame a painting.

The performances are strong on all accounts. Sterling Hayden is great as General Ripper – his cigar-chomping soliloquies on fluoridated water and the Red Menace are priceless. He delivers his madness with a straight face throughout, in a performance that only be described as 'Purity of Essence'.

There are rumors that Kubrick never told Slim Pickens (the B-52 pilot, 'King Kong') this was a satire, so as to get him to play the role straight. This rumor does a great injustice to his performance. Once Pickens starts reading off the contents of the survival kits: 'Two pairs a nylon stockin's. Two pair a prophylactics. Shoot. A fella could have a good time on this in'Vegas.', you realize he was a master of comedic naivete.

George C. Scott plays General Turgison. It took the man who would later play Patton to convincingly sustain this character. The character's precious habit of the military coda compels him to defend Ripper and take pride in the skill of his pilots even as their success means world destruction. The scenes where he stares down the president while stuffing gum in his face are definitely priceless.

But this film belongs to Peter Sellers. As Mandrake he is forced to order Col. `Bat' Guano to shoot open a Coke machine in order to get change to phone the president (to put an end to the nuclear crisis): 'You'll have to answer to the Coca-Cola corporation of Atlanta Georgia'. As The President, he delivers one side of hilarious conversations with his Russian counterpart with great dialogue including the legendary `Gentlemen you can't fight in here – this is the war room!' But as Dr Strangelove he is hilarious – and downright iconic ('Look, Mein Furher — I can VALK!'). The character himself is such a glorious indictment of the US Arms/Space program, wherein former Nazi scientists were recruited, to essentially compete with the Soviets' former Nazi scientists. It is interesting how Seller's Strangelove was eerily evocative (and prescient?) of Kissinger. I am shocked more people did not make note of it during the bombing of Cambodia and US meddling in Chile.

The USAF was going to cooperate with the making of this film until they read the script. The FBI is said to have investigated how they replicated the B-52 Bomber to near perfection. Strategic Air Command are among this film's largest cult base, and it is easy to see why. On a certain level the film indicts the ideology of the cold war and the failure to create safeguards. But policy is not the concern of SAC; it recruits for and highly values dispassionate professionalism. The film portrays SAC as dangerously competent. Skill, ingenuity and *esprit de corps* are precisely what enables the bomber crew to get through.

The end of the Cold War may have taken some of the edge off this film had when we first saw it. It was widely seen as dangerous to American interests when it was first released. However, I once spoke to a Russian journalist friend about him seeing *Strangelove* as a student during the cold war. The Soviets showed the film anticipating a negative impression of the US. Instead, he claims it made him hopeful about the United States, saying that any culture that permitted such a film would also possess enough clarity of vision to prevent nuclear war. Thus *Strangelove* was dangerous and beneficial to both sides. Perhaps, in a small way, it contributed to the thawed relations that ultimately diminished its own relevance. Can you ask for more from a film?

▶▶

EASY RIDER

Date:	1969
Director:	Dennis Hopper
Writer(s):	Peter Fonda, Dennis Hopper and Terry Southern
Runtime(s):	94 minutes
Country:	USA
Language:	English, Spanish

A MAN WENT LOOKING FOR AMERICA AND COULDN'T FIND IT ANYWHERE!

Just how cool is *Easy Rider*?

Apparently we've now reached 'post' post-modern. There is a commercial running in America where a dull office drone is inserted via computer-generated animation into footage of Peter Fonda on his chopper from *Easy Rider*. Turns out the 9 to 5'er is just having a daydream aboard a commuter train because he is high … *on Pepsi*!

People may argue that if Dennis Hopper himself will now do any number of corporate ads, then you could just as easily appropriate his creations also. If this is true, then remember that the movie didn't get lame, the culture did. Rather than diminishing the spirit and era of *Easy Rider*, I think the ad indicts our own, therein making the film more appealing and vital. Shame on the vandals, not the object of their vandalism.

Easy Rider is enjoyable as a moment frozen in time. No matter what hindsight casts upon it, or how it is appropriated and re-interpreted, it is hard to imagine a cooler image then Peter

Fonda in his Captain America Jacket and Dennis Hopper in fringe on the open road. It is no surprise then that something as inert and 'uncool' as a soft drink tries to get cool by association. What happens instead is that putting the two side by side creates such a desperate contrast that Pepsi will never look less cool.

That's how cool it is.

Peter Fonda plays serene Wyatt, while Hopper is a paranoid prophet of the hippies as 'Billy the Kid'. Fonda's lead has a cool, deliberate 'quiet'. It's less intense than subdued and appreciative, like he is taking in everything from the trip. He lets America affect him, not the other way around. Dennis Hopper meanwhile is the sidekick. He is nothing but comment, constantly saying exactly what he thinks. He has little patience for flower children, pretentious intellectuals, coy women, law officers, drunks or rednecks.

A major drug deal goes down, much grass is smoked and the journey eastward begins. The journey towards 'freedom' has always been tied to a drift westward. Convention has it that American freedom hits its apex when you hit the Pacific. These two modern cowboys travel eastward from Los Angeles. They are not seeking freedom, but symbolically testing the limits of freedom by travelling against its current. The two use money from a drug deal to finance their cross-country odyssey.

Along the way the beauty and contradictions of America are witnessed, and discussed in no less than seven campfire chats. Much of the film consists of simply shooting the riders as they travel spiralling highways and bigoted backroads. The beautiful footage by director of photography László Kovács is essential to the trip. They encounter a hippie commune trying to live off the land that is both doomed and liberated by their intentions. In a beautiful irony the bikers are arrested for riding in a fourth of July parade without a permit. The cops throw them into a cell next to an inebriated ACLU lawyer named George, played by Jack Nicholson.

Jack Nicholson is the core of the film. He may not appear until halfway through, but the trip makes much more sense when his face rises up bleary-eyed from the jailhouse cot. He is the innocent man of this group, professional but restless and open to conversion. He represents an America looking to perfect the distance between its ideal and its reality. They let George join them because he tells them he has a helmet. Grinning widely he shows up wearing a gold football helmet with a blue centre stripe.

Even the minor performances are good, including Toni Basil and Karen Black as New Orleans hookers who join the boys on a very disturbing acid trip. The filmmakers used locals whenever possible, and it gives the film much greater texture.

The legitimacy of the film, its relationship to its audience and its now iconic status are a testament to the reciprocal relationship between the era and the filmmakers. They did something right. The film premiered at the 1969 Cannes Film Festival and won the festival's award for the Best Film by a New Director. The film received two Academy Award nominations: Best Original Screenplay (co-authored by Peter Fonda, Dennis Hopper and Terry Southern) and Best Supporting Actor for Jack Nicholson, in this fairly early role.

Easy Rider is the counter-culture assessing its own relationship to the mainstream. As well as co-starring, Fonda produced and Hopper directed (his first effort). It is certainly a more sympathetic and authentic film than Hollywood might have otherwise produced. Far from a sensational 'expose' on biker and drug culture, it was the product of it. As a result the danger in this film does not come from a traditional menace, and that is half its surprise. The finale is sudden, jarring, violent and uncompromising. It's cruel and unfair, and that's the point.

▶▶

EL TOPO

Date:	1970
Director:	Alejandro Jodorowsky
Writer(s):	Alejandro Jodorowsky
Runtime(s):	125 minutes
Country:	Mexico
Language:	Spanish

THE DEFINITIVE CULT SPAGHETTI WESTERN.

There is a cliché I want to see retired, no made illegal – the cliché of comparing something edgy to something bland by claiming 'Such-and-such is like (insert bland item here) on acid'. The only exception would have to be El Topo, which really is a 'Western on acid'. More specifically, this is a spaghetti western on a heavy dose of surrealist artist Luis Buñuel, author Herman Hesse and general 1960s esoterica.

It's obvious why this, the original midnight movie, was embraced by the likes of John Lennon, Dennis Hopper and Timothy Leary. It's a violent, brutal, confusing, occasionally fascinating and allegorical film. Alejandro Jodorowsky infuses the violence of Peckinpah, the style of Leone and the eroticism of Arrabal. Jodorowsky not only writes and directs, he also plays the title role (which translates as 'The Mole'), a mysterious black-clad gunfighter who claims to be God travelling through the desert, initially with his naked seven-year-old son and eventually with two beautiful women.

This film has a very strong flavour of Buñuel particularly in the use of religious themes and stylised absurdity. I think the profoundest parallels may lie in *L'Age D'Or* (1930). To be sure, the ride has moments where sex, violence and landscape are constructed with poetic surrealism. After entering a massacred village, and riding through corpses and carnage, El Topo finds a sole survivor. El Topo then hands his gun over to his son, instructing him to put the man out of his misery. El Topo frees a woman from a despotic colonel whose henchmen have also enslaved and abused a group of Franciscan monks. He strips the colonel, humiliates him and forces him to shoot himself. He later confronts several 'masters' of the desert, including one he covers with dead rabbits and a blind one who is an incredibly fast shooter.

It had to be a true labour of love for Jodorowsky to complete it. As with many self-possessed artists, the very compulsion that drives a project can manifest in self-indulgence. He has after all cast himself as the lead – a powerful avenger, worshipped by women, with not-so-subtle 'God' allusions. Each biblically-titled chapter is constructed episodically, each with the thematic equivalent of a punch line, meant to further highlight the moral preceding it.

Its actual release date not-withstanding, *El Topo* still predates both *The Wild Bunch* (1969) and *Easy Rider* (1969). Filmed over the course of nearly three years, the filmmakers twice were stranded for weeks without supplies or money. This film began production in 1964/65, and wasn't completed until 1968. It was originally set for release in 1968, but was further delayed by distribution problems.

An ongoing dispute between Jodorowsky and producer (and one time Rolling Stones manager) Allen Klein not only delayed the original release, it continues to affect distribution. The only version I was able to get on home video was dubbed into English with Japanese subtitles at the bottom of the screen. It seems most available copies of *El Topo* are grey market dubs taken from Japanese laserdisc. Be prepared for a potential loss in picture quality and the odd Japanese convention of intentionally blurring out all pubic hair. So for full effect (and pubic hair), it is best to try to catch the rare theatrical showing.

Home video technical limitations aside, seeing *El Topo* in a cinema screening also avails you to discussing it with others. Reactions to the movie are all over the map. Many don't like the film. Many find it too pretentious, too disturbing, too violent, too sacrilegious, too scattered. It may be wise to reserve opinions until viewing Jodorowsky's other well-known feature *Holy Mountain* (1973) as well. *Holy Mountain* is lesser known, but commands as much respect among auteurs and fans, and is often described as 'science fiction on Acid'. See a theme here?.

And so calling *El Topo* 'A Western on Acid' can be both praise and criticism, remembering that acid can distort your perception to such a degree that even the back of your hand can fascinate you for hours. As to whether it'd be interesting for others to watch you do it, is the subjective determination viewers bring to films like *El Topo*. Most agree it is art regardless of opinion or interpretations.

▶▶

ENTER THE DRAGON

Date:	1973
Director:	Robert Clouse
Writer(s):	Michael Allin
Runtime(s):	98 minutes, 110 minutes (USA, 25th Anniversary Edition)
Country:	Hong Kong, US
Language:	English

THE FIRST AMERICAN PRODUCED MARTIAL ARTS SPECTACULAR!

Truly, the best of Bruce Lee. A favourite mixture of camp, high adventure, culture clash and martial arts excellence, *Enter the Dragon* survives today as the quintessential Bruce Lee film. It minimises narrative subtlety in order to showcase the actor's inimitable fighting talents. This was the movie that made Bruce Lee a household name in the USA. Sadly, he never lived to see the fame it brought him. He died a month before its release.

The film has every 1970s and martial arts cliché you could hope for to enjoy it ironically. From bad dubbing, to the ultra cool-cat performance of ultra afro'd Jim Kelly, to the funky wakka-wakka guitar music. Also a swooshing then smacking sound effect accompanies every punch and every kick, even if nothing is actually hit, as though every movement breaks the sound barrier. You know from the 'thwacking' sound effect, that each time a contact was made, a leather couch in a sound studio died a little. I also have to say that the legions of nameless henchmen from Kung Fu films generally, and

Bruce Lee movies specifically, are some of the politest characters ever committed to screen. They never double up on their opponent, preferring to patiently wait their turn on the sideline for their allotted beating. The film *Sense and Sensibility* (1995) did not portray as much as etiquette as these fight sequences.

Anyway, the plot: Lee (Bruce Lee) is a James Bond figure sent to stop opium smuggling and finish off the empire of Asian crime lord Han (Kien Shih) at his annual international martial arts tournament on a remote island near Hong Kong. The tournament is a showcase for Han's philosophy, as well as a convenient recruitment method. In fact Han's private island is a dictatorship; one in which he 'lives like a king', and receives adulation and fascist salutes of raised, punching fists from the competitors.

Among other men who come to Han's island are the Americans Roper (John Saxon) and Williams (Jim Kelly). They are white and black respectively, their backgrounds offered in flashback sequences. One is wanted by the mob and the other by the police.

Lee has come to Han's island primarily to do the secret-agent thing but of course, as is always part of the Kung Fu picture formula, the mission is also personal. Lee finds out that his sister committed suicide to avoid capture by Han's right hand man, O'Hara (Robert Wall). He realises that he must simultaneously defeat the goon and the crime lord for very different reasons.

Lee is frequently shown in slow motion, catching his rapid-fire actions as he fights O'Hara, numerous cavern guards, a variety of tournament competitors, and finally, Han himself. If you see only one movie this year where a man with knives for fingers gets the daylights kicked out of him in a hall of mirrors, let it be this one.

Could Lee really beat 50 opponents in quick succession? Could anyone? The suspension of disbelief necessary is achieved by the potent physical artistry of the performer, and not computer generated post-effects. Director Robert Clouse rose to the occasion, thanks entirely to a very charismatic star. Lee does it all with authority and skill, with bare hands and nunchuka.

Western cinema had never before portrayed Asian males as virile and physically superior to Westerners. Lee's strengths coincided with shifts in racial perceptions brought on in no small part by the shock that the defeats in Vietnam had on the Western psyche. There is a deliberate and revealing juxtaposition between Lee and the Westerners in this film. When the Williams character is asked why he wouldn't notice being defeated he replies, 'I'll be too busy looking good.' Conversely, after winning every contest, the topless and blood-tasting Lee provides a far more convincing image of physical potency than the sexually active Roper and Williams ever do. Likewise these themes are emphasised in the scene where the British agent, Braithwaite (Geoffrey Weeks), briefs Lee. He offers Lee a drink, which the ascetic fighter declines. The scene also confirms Lee's disdain for firearms ('Any bloody fool can pull a trigger.') The contrast in vitality and integrity between the ultra-fit Asian Lee and the middle aged, bespectacled European agent could not have been more evident if Braithwaite was wearing a powdered wig.

In scenes that both foreshadow an emerging genre, and affirm Lee's legacy within it, the actor takes down future martial arts icons Sammo Hung (in the opening fight scene) and Jackie Chan (in the tunnel) in this film. *Enter the Dragon* deserves cult status as a timeless martial arts classic, a cultural artefact and as the swan song for a brilliant performer who died too young.

▶▶

FASTER, PUSSY CAT KILL! KILL!

Date:	1966
Director:	Russ Meyer
Writer(s):	Russ Meyer (story), Jack Moran
Runtime(s):	83 minutes
Country:	US
Language:	English

GO-GO FOR A WILD RIDE WITH THE ACTION GIRLS!

When you say 'Russ Meyer', you know exactly what you are getting: busty chicks, slang-laden dialogue, low-grade violence, fast cars and tragic consequences. Meyer films are guilty pleasures – unpretentious, dated, fun, exploitative schlock. Of the many films in his oeuvre, *Faster, Pussy Cat Kill! Kill!* is his *Citizen Kane*. Enjoy this little gem guiltlessly, because to be honest, compared to contemporary fare like *Charlie's Angels: Full Throttle* (2003), it's *The Tempest*.

The film opens on vertical audio patterns vacillating in sync to an over-stimulated narrator pontificating about the violent nature of the female gender, and the connection between eroticism and murder. The peculiar opening then cuts to a dizzying collage of go-go dancers wiggling with reverse cuts to the head of a male spectator floating in a black background howling with both anger and arousal 'Yeah, baby!' and 'Faster! Faster! Go! Go!'

Three strippers, Varla (Tura Satana), Rosie (Haji) and Billie (Lori Williams), cruise the California desert, each in a distinctive imported roadster (because carpooling would have just been too 'square'). Rosie is a brunette kitten with hints of lesbianism and an even more ambiguous accent. Billie is a blonde 'good girl' who breaks into go-go dancing fits for no apparent reason. But it is Tura Satana's dominatrix in driving gloves, Varla, that makes the film iconic. She is busty, vampish, violent and sassy while never once besmirching her perfect 'Betty Page' make-up and hair.

They cross paths with an all-American couple, Tommy (Ray Barlow) and Linda (Susan Bernard). Tommy is a car enthusiast and a 'good kid'. His strong jaw and plaid ensemble reassure us of his American-teen wholesomeness, while the unremarkable girlfriend Linda pretty much only exists as a showcase for abuse from others.

Drag racing ensues, which leads to a fight and inevitably the murder of Tommy by Varla. They leave his corpse in his car and, for reasons unknown but to Meyers, knock Linda unconscious and take her with them.

Down the road the femmes fatale learn from a service station attendant, who pumps exposition as well as fuel, that there's an isolated household nearby with a crippled old man (Stuart Lancaster), his shotgun, two sons and supposedly a large stash of money. One son (Dennis Busch) is a big strong lug with the subtle nickname 'vegetable', while the other, Kirk (Paul Trinka), is the closest this movie comes to a sympathetic character.

The would-be heist is both thwarted and aided by the cinematic axiom that those who live in seclusion are sexually deviant, socially inept, intellectually deficient and emotionally troubled. The crippled guy's back-story is almost interesting enough that you care what happens to this damaged family, almost. Meyer's trio won't let that last, however, as they karate chop, cat fight and seduce their way towards the money.

Remember this is the Playboy era of 'innocent smut'. The camera may fixate on the strippers' bodies, but there's no hint of actual sex, 'kinky' or otherwise. Innuendo rules the script. It is less actual dialogue then merely 1966 slang exchanged at tennis-match speed. Everything is subtext for something else: sex is an extension of violence, violence an outlet for sex. Cars represent both sex and violence, and are the weapon of choice in most of the film's murders.

If you aren't comfortable simply enjoying 60s trash films and need to legitimate the experience, you could adopt the revisionist view of the film, often promoted in academic circles: that it contains valuable cultural significance in portraying the power of female sexuality on men. The women are the offenders, physically stronger and more cunning than the naive guys in this film. Varla especially is a sexy, immensely violent murder machine. Unfortunately that involves equating (and therefore justifying) violence as power, and pretending that the dominatrix fantasy isn't simply one of the many flavours of male fetish. So if you want to cultivate a fetish without guilt, choose one that can be also embraced as a 'feminist oppositional reading'. Or you could just dig the film.

▶▶

FIGHT CLUB

Date:	1999
Director:	David Fincher
Writer(s):	Chuck Palahniuk (novel), Jim Uhls (screenplay)
Runtime(s):	139 minutes
Country:	US, Germany
Language:	English

MISCHIEF. MAYHEM. SOAP.

Regarding *Fight Club* there are two camps: those who consider it a disturbing celebration of homoerotic brutality, and those who have actually seen it. Ostensibly, it's a movie about the creation of a 'fight club', where guys beat the crap out of one another bare knuckled so they can feel real again. *Fight Club* is also a wild ride in which some abstract concepts are explored with visceral intensity. It's about existential dread, consumerism and the refusal to live a numb life. And it's a movie that would rather show than tell.

The tone is set even before the formation of the club, which is a mere extension of the film's greater themes. We meet the narrator Jack (Ed Norton), who is suffering a general malaise compounded by insomnia or, as he refers to himself, 'not deprived of sleep, but deprived of rest'. He has the soul-challenging job of investigating accidents for which his automobile company employer is culpable, using an equation that measures the cost effectiveness of out-of-court settlements versus a product recall.

Jack seeks to reconnect with authentic human emotion by joining a variety of support groups for people with terminal illnesses. It is at one such group for survivors of testicular cancer that he meets Robert Paulson (Meat Loaf). In the naked, unmediated pain of others, he finds solace. Briefly.

He becomes indignant when he encounters the same woman, Marla Singer (Helena Bonham Carter), at every support group (even testicular cancer). Her insincerity as a 'tourist' diminishes his sense of authenticity in the experience of each group, and his restlessness returns.

While on a business trip, he strikes up a conversation with a fellow passenger named Tyler Durden, an unkempt Brad Pitt who ironically travels selling his own brand of soap. When Jack's condo is firebombed he calls Tyler, who invites him to move in with him in an enormous, dilapidated mansion 'where nothing works', and the two of them have a blast, hitting golf balls and staying up late.

Jack stays with his day job, but also helps Tyler with his business, making designer soap out of human fat stolen from liposuction clinics. They take it to high-end department stores and sell it for 20 bucks a bar. 'We're selling their fat asses back to them,' Jack snickers.

Jack and Tyler hang out in a seedy bar, and get to punching each other out in the parking lot. Other guys observe them, are really impressed, and end up forming 'fight club', where guys take turns beating each other up. The idea spreads, and eventually a movement is formed, wherein the dispossessed gather to exorcise their quiet desperation, by beating and being beaten into bloody pulps.

Marla shows up and starts sleeping with Tyler. But it's only sex; she prefers the company of Jack, who still remains indignant.

Meanwhile the club has morphed into a kind of hyper-disciplined paramilitary cult. We learn that Tyler has been secretly visiting dozens of cities, setting up dozens of fight clubs, and recruiting hundreds of terrorists in order to promote chaos and acts of violence against 'corporate art'. The ultimate goal is to recruit enough people on the inside to blow up a few key office buildings, thereby destroying all the financial records in the country.

It might seem a difficult sell to argue that a major US studio film staring one of the biggest stars in the world can be classified as subversive. But it is precisely that this audacious little broadside to consumer culture could be created using the apparatus of a major studio that makes it subversive. And casting Meat Loaf in a heartbreakingly sympathetic role would be enough subversion for any film. Director David Fincher clearly used whatever cachet he had accrued on hits like *Seven* (1995) to shepherd a little-known novel written by auto mechanic Chuck Palahniuk through the gauntlet of potential studio meddling. That a director at the top of his game and an actor so iconic he is practically a brand himself would do this film lends a certain credibility to the risk involved.

It is worth noting that *Fight Club* came out during an excellent year for American cinema. 1999 also saw *Being John Malkovich*, *Magnolia, Rushmore, Three Kings* and *American Beauty*. Attribute it to end of the millennium psychosis, or the fact that the studios had exhausted every trend imaginable, requiring a brief 'films that don't suck' fad. Whatever the reason, each project heightened expectations and affirmed the plausible commercial viability of the next. All the aforementioned were innovative and raw films, taking risks in both form and/or content. Each reflected weariness in America of a mediated, mindlessly overgrown, corporate sanitised, toxified, greedy, self-absorbed, compass-less culture.

What separates *Fight Club* from the other innovative films and enabled it to develop cult film status is its sheer frenetic energy. Even as it passed from second-run theatres into video release, the film lingered as a popular, weekend, midnight-movie staple. It was able to strike a chord at the right moment. It remained smart, intense and hilarious at the same time. Hilarious? A brutal hyper-intense movie funny? Yes, sometimes painfully funny. And even if the last act of the film isn't believable, it just doesn't matter. Because the film is deconstructing itself from the start, daring you to notice it's a movie all along. At one point while Jack is trying to convince Marla to leave the city by bus, a couple of cinemas are visible with signs announcing the movies *Seven Years in Tibet* (1997, starring Brad Pitt), *The People vs. Larry Flynt* (1996, starring Norton) and *The Wings of the Dove* (1997, starring Carter). It doesn't care – it wants you to question the media continuum.

In a sea of self-referential, post-modern films, *Fight Club* was able to distinguish itself and gain a loyal following because it explores cynical detachment, debunks it and asks 'what's next'? When Tyler and Jack meet there is this exchange:

Tyler Durden:	**You're very clever.**
Jack:	**Thanks.**
Tyler Durden:	**How's that working out for you?**
Jack:	**What?**
Tyler Durden:	**Being clever.**

This exchange is a wonderful taunt to the audience. The director knows the audience is in on the joke. He does not dispute it. But it challenges how gratifying that really is. The essence of the film asks, 'What if any meaning can be constructed once we have determined we are not in charge of our own lives?'

▶▶

► FREAKS

Date:	1932
Director:	Tod Browning
Writer(s):	Clarence Aaron 'Tod' Robbins (short story 'Spurs'), Al Boasberg (uncredited), Willis Goldbeck (uncredited), Leon Gordon (uncredited), Edgar Allan Woolf (uncredited)
Runtime(s):	64 minutes
Country:	USA
Language:	English

THE STRANGEST ... THE MOST STARTLING
HUMAN STORY EVER SCREENED ...
ARE YOU AFRAID TO BELIEVE
WHAT YOUR EYES SEE?

No matter how you approach it, *Freaks* is a peculiar piece of cinema. The title refers to people who make a living off their physical abnormalities on the carnival circuit. Not only are these 'freaks' the subject of the film, but also such performers make-up the majority of the cast. The graphic depictions of these people are fascinating enough, but the fact the film was made in the early 1930s makes it even more extraordinary. It simply does not fit any genre, and one has to admire the audacity of making it.

The plot, though simple, is powerfully executed within the social microcosm of the sideshow circus. A midget named Hans (Harry Earles) falls in love with a beautiful trapeze artist named Cleopatra (Olga Baclanova). In order to win Cleopatra's heart, Hans sacrifices the love of his long-time

77

girlfriend and fellow midget Frieda (Daisy Earles). Cleopatra is in love with Strongman Hercules (Henry Victor) and repulsed by Hans until she discovers that Hans is wealthy. Cleopatra and Hercules conspire to gain Hans' inheritance by having her marry him and kill him shortly thereafter. During the wedding reception. Cleopatra is appalled to discover that in marrying a freak, you become one and are expected to live among them. They ritualistically welcome her into their fold by chanting 'one of us' and offering a sip from their communal goblet. Disgusted, Cleopatra refuses and taunts Hans, humiliating him in front of his surrogate family.

The freaks then discover Cleopatra's plot to poison Hans for the inheritance. Within their code of loyalty they exact revenge for the stricken Hans. On a dark and stormy night they chase down Cleopatra and Hercules, killing him and mutilating her into what we later discover is a legless, scarred, voiceless side show attraction called 'Chickenlady'.

It was not surprisingly a commercial failure. The film was made just before the potent Code era in which the US government oversaw the enforcement of strict censorship rules. The combination of graphic depictions of physical abnormalities, sex, violence and perceived exploitation led to a ban for several decades. Its reputation endured nonetheless, and we all know there is nothing like a ban to tantalise an audience and engender cult status.

It may also be a mistake to label the film as horror. It is certainly a morality tale, and possibly a thriller, but the horror label seems applied solely on the basis of the presence of real carnival 'freaks' in the cast. If anything the film diminishes in shock value as it progresses. The more screen time devoted to the freaks, the more desensitised and sympathetic the audience becomes to them. Which is antithetical to the nature of exploitation and the conventions of horror.

I do not mean to exaggerate the artfulness of the film itself. The storyline is simple and the dialogue is flat. The production values are pure B-movie level, even by the standards of 1932, and the acting by the 'normal' actors is abysmal. But ironically the 'freaks', who are essentially playing themselves, are the most natural of the actors in the film.

I disagree with criticising Browning for using of real 'freaks' in the film for two reasons. Using them is the only way the film could work, even today. Also there is no disrespect paid to the actors in any way. It was brave of Browning to not only present these people on camera, but present them with dignity. The film reflects realistic reactions and social mores. It's an indictment of society at large that the 'freaks' who would likely have been ostracised and even institutionalised in the outside world create a functional collective in their sideshow company. One with the companionship, loyalty and comfort so often lacking among 'normals'. At first the freaks seem grotesque and repellent, but it's incredible how quickly they become sympathetic, likable characters.

Harry Earles as Hans is certainly an interesting 'lead' character. Between the poor audio track, his size-affected voice and a heavy German accent, I have no idea what he is saying 90 per cent of the time. But the character conveys real heartbreak and disappointment by the betrayal of his 'normal' wife. A little person who is also an aristocrat makes the character a refreshingly complex figure, as he is forced to reconcile his high status and privilege with the biases related to his condition.

I believe *Freaks* cult appeal runs deeper than simple fascination with and exploitation of the grotesque.

Condemning this film as exploitative may be too simplistic, for it dismisses a rather groundbreaking bit of cinema. Some may perceive it (and even enjoy it) as such, but that doesn't necessarily make it true.

▶▶

FRITZ THE CAT

Date:	1972
Director:	Ralph Bakshi
Writer(s):	Ralph Bakshi, Robert Crumb (comic book)
Runtime(s):	78 minutes
Country:	US
Language:	English

HE'S X-RATED AND ANIMATED!

There was a time when the very idea of sex and violence in a cartoon was so antithetical it would draw audiences on the novelty alone. *Fritz the Cat* was the first of its kind to receive an X rating from the MPAA. Audiences flocked, making it a midnight-movie staple and a forerunner for cult cinemas as a recognised and marketable genre. It broke ground for animation as a subversive and adult art form. We are now quite accustomed to adult-themed japanimation and can watch cartoons like *South Park*, which on a weekly basis exceed the boundaries pressed by *Fritz*. But it is important to take the film in its historical context before judging it too harshly. Though it may appear dated, the very things that made it audacious for its time serve as an important document to the effort to exceed limitations. You name the hot topic of the late 60s, Ralph Bakshi went after it.

Based on Robert Crumb's groundbreaking underground comic, Bakshi took Fritz – an oversexed, cool and hip character – and tried to paint a portrait of 60s America and its shortcomings. He attempted to shock with both a raunchy sex comedy and biting political drama. However, the film, like the counterculture that inspired it, doesn't succeed on either level.

We meet our hero Fritz the cat as he begins his descent into proverbial madness. The cast of characters is meant to be representative of race, colour and creed, all in the guise of different animals. The story is simple enough – Fritz the cat is a college student in New York, out to get laid. At the park he meets three girls, who he impresses enough with his hackneyed 'philosophy' to entice them to an apartment for sex. From there, Fritz goes on a series of misadventures, running from the cops (who are represented as pigs), burning his college dorm, winding up stoned in Harlem with the crows (the film's depiction of blacks), starting a riot and ultimately meeting up with the 'real' revolution – a crypto-fascist gang plotting to blow up a power plant somewhere in the American Southwest.

Like Fritz, the film is confused about what it wants. Overall it has a 'groovy' late 60s/early 70s feel to it. Unfortunately, it drags severely in most places. It skips around from vignette to vignette without any real theme to connect them other than the sex/drugs/rock and roll overtones.

The most important break from tradition is that *Fritz* is written for adults. But beyond the fact that animated characters are naked and have sex, Fritz broke other 'rules' of animation. Most of the backgrounds are minimalist, with only line drawings instead of the rich 'Disney' detail. Bakshi overlays his animation with colour gels, reinforcing the 'psychedelic' world that Fritz sometimes lives in. There are parts of the film in which the characters react against a black background with few, if any, further detailing. Instead music adds depth to the animated scenes, and Bakshi uses it extremely well.

Bakshi (and Crumb in the comics) pulls no punches when he depicts Fritz living the life of a 'radical', oblivious of the consequences of his actions until it's too late. Walt never had the guts to make such a stand. However, the cartoon's use of racial stereotypes is inappropriate in today's society (and rightly so).

Fritz the Cat is a viable historical landmark movie, and should be viewed not only by animation buffs, but also as a means of understanding how the 60s were defined in their own time.

▶▶

GET CARTER

Date:	1971
Director:	Mike Hodges
Writer(s):	Ted Lewis (novel), Mike Hodges
Runtime(s):	112 minutes
Country:	UK
Language:	English

WHAT HAPPENS WHEN A PROFESSIONAL KILLER VIOLATES THE CODE? GET CARTER!

Based on Ted Lewis' pulp novel *Jack's Return Home*, Mike Hodges took an interesting scenario and vastly improved upon the material. The film follows Jack Carter (Michael Caine), a no-nonsense right-hand man to a top London gangster (playwright John Osborne as a sinister Mr. Big, Cyril Kinnear). Carter is well known for his ruthlessness. His brother has died in what is alleged to be a drink-driving accident, and Carter goes home to Newcastle for the funeral. He suspects murder and he is right. Slowly and surely the plot reveals the ghastly details. As Jack uncovers the truth, anyone with the slightest connection begins to regret it.

Hampering Carter's investigations are Cyril Kinnear's representatives from London. The boss doesn't appreciate his links with the Newcastle mob being damaged. Initially they try to negotiate and placate Carter. When they attempt to buy him off, it's too late. When they resort to using force, they are no match for Carter's steely resolve.

Get Carter is often called a 'gangster' movie, and though it involves gangsters as characters, it doesn't really fit the conventions of that genre. It's more of a Jacobean revenge drama, set against the backdrop of petty organised crime in a northern British town.

At the height of the 'anti-hero' movement in cinema, Caine's Carter is an amoral man on a moral crusade. He adheres to the only ethos of crime syndicates: money. How many times in a gangster film have we heard a killer before a mob execution utter some variation on 'it's nothing personl; its business' to their victim? But for Carter it becomes personal. When it becomes personal, his motivation makes him less pragmatic and entirely unpredictable.

Carter is not a decent man. Either by habit or necessity he is methodical and cruel. It is interesting that he does not ascribe any motivation to others apart from money. When an associate is brutally beaten helping him, Carter coldly throws him money for his suffering. A moral hero would not be so steeped in the methods and manner of the underworld element. A moral hero's actions are measured by decency, thereby becoming half measures, stunted and hesitant. Carter is Hamlet without the hesitation. Carter's motives and methods are absolute. He has singularity of purpose. His is total war.

The use of provincial locations in the early 1970s was almost unique in British cinema. One look at the Newcastle of *Get Carter* makes it easy to see why – bleak and dreary, it makes you speculate that suicide might have been the cause of Carter's brother's death. Moving the setting to Newcastle was a brilliant choice on the part of Hodges, as he created a milieu perfect for the dank events unfolding on the screen. The almost vérité style and the local flavour of disheartened blue-collar 1970s Newcastle gives it all the atmosphere it needs.

Some of the film is also darkly funny and wonderfully subtle. The ease with which Caine has phone sex with Britt Eckland in front of his landlady is priceless. Also wonderful is the scene in which Caine, naked with a shotgun, dispatches would be assassins from a council flat.

I would recommend listening very carefully to the dialogue. Not because it is remarkable, but because you can't hear *anything*! The sound quality is very poor on every print I have seen. It seems at times that the frequent long shots are accompanied by even further placement of the microphone. And even medium shots have the audio quality of a mike wrapped in duct tape, placed in a cardboard box.

That said, I will take any and all technical limitations to the wrong-minded, budget-bloated US remake with Sylvester Stallone (*Get Carter*, 2001). I hesitate to mention the remake except in the necessity to warn potential viewers of mistaking this bad film for the original. The remake even managed to attract Caine for a cameo. But then what bad movie doesn't have a Michael Caine cameo?

If you wish to expand upon the tone of a film like *Get Carter* without defaming its memory, I recommend the similarly gritty *Croupier* (1998) also made by Mike Hodges.

▶▶

GIMME SHELTER

Date:	1970
Directors:	Albert Maysles, David Maysles
Runtime(s):	91 minutes
Country:	US
Language:	English

THE MUSIC THAT THRILLED THE WORLD ... AND THE KILLING THAT STUNNED IT!

Following them on a 1969 US tour, *Gimme Shelter* catches the Rolling Stones at their absolute apex. Interspersed with the live performance footage, we see the negotiations between lawyers and promoters who must find a last-minute alternate venue for a free concert scheduled in San Francisco. They decide on Altamonte Speedway. All events in the film lead to this event.

Intended to be the West Coast answer to *Woodstock*, the word 'Altamonte' has come to mean to live entertainment what 'Waterloo' means to French Cavalry. The speedway owner offered his venue hoping to generate free publicity, and I am sure he got more than he could have imagined. During the concert, the film crew actually captured the stabbing to death of a concert attendee by a Hell's Angels member not 30 feet from the Rolling Stones' performance stage.

If a cautionary tale can also be exhilarating, this is it. If *Woodstock* makes you nostalgic for a bygone era, *Gimme Shelter* will remind you why it all had to end. The Altamonte concert was a fiasco of good intentions, cynical promotion and dangerous naivety. In the spirit of keeping the event 'free', the promoters allowed members of the Hell's Angels motorcycle gang to provide 'security'. They made the equally dubious choice of providing the Angels with 'all the beer they want' in lieu of money. It kind of defeats the purpose when 'security' knocks out the lead singer in mid-performance. This happens to Marty Balin of Jefferson Airplane. When Grace Slick criticises the action, a biker hops on Marty's mike and tries to argue with her.

Gimme Shelter does feature some big acts, including Jefferson Airplane, The Grateful Dead, Neil Young and Crazy Horse and Tina Turner and Ike Turner doing a rendition of the classic Otis Redding song 'I've Been Loving You Too Long'. But this is not much of a traditional 'concert film'; rather the poorly-mixed soundtrack captures the experience and imperfection of live performance that may frustrate record executives, but keeps bootleg recordings in demand. The film understands its obligation to the 'experience' of the concert, and not necessarily the music.

The film presents an interesting relationship to its subject matter by opening with Charlie Watts and Mick Jagger viewing rushes of the film in an editing suite and showing their responses throughout. The film starts with them viewing the infamous Altamonte death scene. The foregone conclusion creates a lingering doom that inspires a kind of alertness for the audience. Any enjoyment of the concert footage is tainted by the impending death. One after another, the decisions leading up to the concert gain an eerie foreboding. Viewing the film with hindsight, anticipating the festival's tragic conclusion, one wonders how any other outcome could have been expected.

Rarely does a performer become an established icon while they are still at the top of their game. This film catches that intersection in Mick Jagger's career perfectly. But it is as important to show how people are affected by a performance as much as to show the performers themselves. Nearly all of the Altamonte footage is shot from behind the band to feature the audience, which, as it turns out, is the stroke of genius that makes this movie so special. At earlier venues we see Mick literally preening as the centre of attention. At Altamonte he cannot contain his audience. The audience is the true 'star' of the film. Events supersede Mick – he tries to respond, but he is no leader.

Critics such as Pauline Kael and Vincent Canby derided the film as exploitative. Some charged that the filmmakers, if not complicit in the lethal chaos, were at least exploiting it. Or you can say 'don't blame the messenger' and draw your own conclusions.

The incident portrayed reveals the kind of fascinating moral ambiguity that only happens in real life. And it is a well-made documentary that does not interrupt the ambiguity by seeking to resolve it. The film captures that the stabbing victim clearly had drawn a gun. Mick's response is hard to discern. On the one hand there is shock and recrimination, and on the other the very real possibility the victim could have been him.

Gimme Shelter is many things; a great rock 'n' roll film, a well-constructed documentary and a challenging mix of voyeurism and dark fascination. Above all, it is a glimpse into the end of an era. The most telling scene may not be the infamous stabbing, but the final sequence showing the audience straggling home next morning. Like tired refugees from the waning decade, they walk tired and bleary eyed into a cold, unwelcome dawn.

▶▶

THE GOOD, THE BAD
AND THE UGLY

Date:	1966
Director:	Sergio Leone
Writer(s):	Sergio Leone (story and screenplay), Luciano Vincenzoni (story and screenplay), Agenore Incrocci screenplay) and Furio Scarpelli (screenplay)
Runtime(s):	161 minutes, 186 minutes (France, dubbed version), 182 minutes (Spain), 180 minutes (UK, re-release)
Country:	Italy/ Spain
Language:	Italian

FOR THREE MEN THE CIVIL WAR WASN'T HELL.
IT WAS PRACTICE!

Bene! Bene! Bene! Sergio Leone is the master craftsman of the 'Spaghetti Western' and *The Good, the Bad and the Ugly* is his masterpiece. An Italian director shooting Spain as the American West could not help but invent a genre. Sergio Leone reflects the old world taking a fresh and distinct account of the new. It is Europe in a reciprocal relationship with America. The American West is here for the first time portrayed outside of the USA and therefore outside its sensibilities and biases (and some would say 'accuracy'.

As *The Godfather* series similarly did with the mobster genre, Leone doesn't make a Western so much as an opera applied to a Western backdrop. The drama is painted with broad strokes on a Spanish location that could not be less realistically the US Southwest, if it were a canvas backdrop on an operatic stage. Within grand themes he then applies a kind of 'stylised realism'.

The music is iconic: Ennio Morricone's famously eerie score (you've heard it before) is as distinctive as the lead actors in this film. Clint Eastwood ('the good'), Lee Van Cleef ('the bad') and the ineffable Eli Wallach ('the ugly') are some of the best examples of face-casting you'll ever see. The motivations are basic: 'greed', 'revenge', 'sociopathic'. Yet the characters are complex, the morality ambiguous and the back-stories are elaborate. Leone's films blend the opposition of never less than three protagonists, requiring twisting plot mechanisations, shifting alliances and a classic 'Mexican stand-off'.

Clint Eastwood is icy, cool and quietly efficient. He turns in accused criminals for bounties and frees them before they are hung. Lee Van Cleef may be as cool as Eastwood, but he has a slicker, smoother and, dressed in black, decidedly more evil persona than Eastwood. But Eli Wallach, as Tuco, is the most memorable. Tuco is the most complex and sympathetic of the trio. He has an outlaw persona with traits of humanity that do not make him an entirely bad person. In his moral ambiguity and charming pragmatism, Tuco is the wild card, the axis upon which the two other forces are balanced, and ultimately tip.

It is, in many ways, the most comprehensive western ever made. Leone, as familiar with the myth of the American West as he was aware of its near exhaustion, not only revived the genre but took it places Hollywood had never dared take it before. He made TV actor Clint Eastwood into an international superstar, and in the process invented a character – the gun slinging 'man with no name' – who embodied the Western's next generation: tough, morally ambiguous and clouded in a mystery unknown to the likes of Gene Autrey and John Wayne.

Leone directs with panache and intelligence, two qualities you rarely find in the same movie. The two other films in the trilogy, *A Fistful of Dollars* (1964) and *For a Few Dollars More* (1965) are grand accomplishments with many of the same elements as this one, but with *The Good, the Bad and the Ugly*, Leone has broadened his scope – literally and figuratively. He uses every last inch of his Cinemascope-enhanced frames, particularly in the final scene: the best shootout ever put on screen. The narrative stretches across two-and-a-half hours, during which the characters manage to develop without compromising their archetypal power.

The civil war backdrop provides for necessary plot machinations. But it also offers inexplicable desert warfare and the swarthiest confederates in the history of cinema. Maybe it was Garibaldi's army, maybe the location was meant to be Palermo. And maybe, before you let the question go any further, you get one more burst of the coolest theme music ever, and you just don't care.

▶▶

THE HARDER THEY COME

Date:	1973
Director:	Perry Henzell
Writer(s):	Perry Henzell, Trevor D. Rhone
Runtime(s):	120 minutes
Country:	Jamaica
Language:	English

WITH A PIECE IN HIS HAND
HE TAKES ON THE MAN!

Few movie soundtracks have changed the face of popular music more than the one for *The Harder They Come*, which single-handedly put reggae on the map, paving the way for Bob Marley's breakthrough album a year later. Billed as 'Jamaica's very first feature-length film', it shouldered the responsibility of introducing the country to a world so unfamiliar with Jamaica, it is one of the few English-language films where English subtitles were deemed necessary.

While it was ultimately the songs – 'You Can Get It If You Really Want', 'Many Rivers To Cross', 'Pressure Drop', the title track, among other classics (music by Toots and the Maytals) – that established the film's reputation, *The Harder They Come* remains a powerful testament to their deeper cultural meaning.

It is a social commentary, political manifesto and comedy all rolled-into-one. Singer-songwriter Jimmy Cliff stars as a country naïf (Ivan Martin) who arrives in Kingston with little money and no prospects, determined to be a famous musician. Once there, he faces corruption at every turn, from a monopolistic producer who will only pay him $20 a song, to a missionary church that peddles 'The Word' and a corrupt police force. Desperation tempts him to the ganja trade, and he finally achieves notoriety by shooting a few cops in self-defence. He goes underground; even as his single climbs to the top of the charts. Ivan's rise to fame begins to parallel that of Rhygin, a famous Jamaican gunman of the 1940s. He begins to imagine himself a classic anti-hero, a kind of spaghetti western gunman.

Henzell and co-writer Trevor Rhone adapted the original script for Cliff to play the lead role. Like Ivan, Cliff migrated from the country to the city as a youth, and faced similar obstacles breaking into the music business.

Its technical limitations only enhance its gritty tale of hard men and harder times. Shot in documentary style, the camera stays tuned to the shantytown squalor of the Kingston slums, where people are shown sifting through beachside garbage heaps, looking for scraps of food. Layered with biting ironies, Henzell's story lands forceful blows to the capital-A Authority that poisons every social and religious institution in the city.

Henzell has talked about his obsession with capturing this reality, as well as the delight Jamaican audiences felt when they finally saw themselves on film. Henzell claims the film was 'made for illiterates, slum dwelling illiterates everywhere', even though the film was never expected to be viewed outside Jamaica. Henzell has discussed how the film broadened to a cult audience: he claims that because the film is so local, so real, it also fascinates educated people who want a glimpse into another world. Films so often appeal to a wider audience by generalising the human experience, this one does so by its specific authenticity. The sincerity in its expression, the very particularity of portrayal garners a strong response, even three worlds away.

'Cross many rivers' if you have to, but see this film.

▶▶

HAROLD AND MAUDE

Date:	1971
Director:	Hal Ashby
Writer(s):	Colin Higgins
Runtime(s):	91 minutes
Country:	US
Language:	English

THEY WERE MEANT TO BE.
BUT EXACTLY WHAT THEY WERE MEANT TO BE
IS NOT QUITE CLEAR.

When polling people as to their cult film list, *Harold and Maude* was most frequently named first. If not, then the person would invariably chastise themselves upon realising they had forgotten it.

It's a beautiful movie with great hope and deep trust in its audience. It is defiantly sentimental, confronting very dark themes and then sweetly, irrefutably negating them in the person of Maude.

Harold and Maude contains one of the best opening scenes in Hollywood history. Harold Chasen (Bud Cort) is a repressed young man whose main outlets are attending funerals of people he didn't know and the staging of elaborate pseudo-suicides, much to the annoyance of his wealthy and controlling mother (Vivian Pickles). By his own admission, he has tried to commit suicide 15 times – including the opening sequence where he puts on the Cat Stevens record 'Don't Be Shy', walks over to a stool and hangs himself. His mother walks in and, entirely used to his suicides, casually uses the phone to cancel a hair appointment and leaves. On other occasions Harold smears himself with fake blood and allows his mother to find him in her shower, or he floats facedown in the family pool as she takes a leisurely swim.

When Harold's mother gives him a new Jaguar sportster, the following shot reveals a priceless close-up of Harold's mischievous grin followed by the lighting of a blowtorch.

Mother runs Harold through a gamut of institutional influences – the Church, mental health and even the military – until she decides upon marriage as a solution. She signs Harold up for 'computer dating'. When Harold's mother introduces him to one of a series of his 'blind dates' he has just finished transforming the Jaguar into a hearse sportscar. On another such 'date', he appears to be listening intently, until he suddenly pulls out a large cleaver and hacks off his fake left arm.

Then at one of the funerals, Harold meets Maude (Ruth Gordon), an eccentric 79-year-old non-conformist. What follows is one of the funniest and most touching pairings in screen history, exploring love, death and the importance of living. Maude has no driver's license, no car of her own, but drives everywhere. She 'borrows' things from others, including cars, to 'remind them that stuff is here today, gone tomorrow'. When a motorcycle cop (Tom Skerritt) pulls over a 'borrowed' car, Maude and Harold merely take off on his motorcycle. Some days they just go to a salvage yard.

There is a marvellous two-second shot that entirely justifies and emboldens Maude as a survivor who truly decides to make it count. To her, order and civilisation rightfully cannot be trusted. She has no time for guilt – one earns their survival by what they do after their second chance, not before. Existing is not the same as living, and not living is a fate far worse than death.

Harold announces to his mother that he is marrying Maude. Then follow scenes of advice from a therapist, an army-general uncle and, most memorably, a priest whose declaration of 'this fills me with revulsion', replete with references to Maude's 'sagging breasts' and 'flabby buttocks', is hilariously unflinching.

If you are not moved by the closing sequence, please have someone place a mirror near your mouth and test for breathing. Having surprised Maude with a party for her eightieth birthday, Maude informs Harold she has already made plans, namely that she already took the pills. The strains of Cat Steven's 'Trouble' glide over scenes of Harold rushing Maude to the hospital, the staff trying to save her, Harold weeping as he drives his car to the cliffs and sends it over, crashing to the rocks below. In the final scene Harold walks away from the precipice playing a banjo Maude had given him.

A staple for video-store 'cult favourite' shelves and midnight-movie showings for 30 years, this film had its biggest success in Minneapolis – where it ran, in the mid-70s, for three years at the old Westgate Theatre in Edina. The theatre then closed its doors, realising maybe that this could never be topped. At it's 1,000th showing Ruth Gordon (Maude) visited in person.

The supporting characters are all top drawer. Charles Tyner's performance as Uncle Victor is a fantastic walking (barely) indictment of the US military mindset in the late Vietnam War era. Vivian Pickles should have been nominated for an Oscar for her priceless portrayal of Harold's mother ('Harold, please!'). You can't help but feel a little sorry for Tom Skerritt's police officer. He just can't win, but according to Maude 'that's the curse of a government job!'

It is the leads, however, that are so marvellous it has become impossible to separate them from their roles. Bud Cort was so identified with 'Harold' it may have cast a shadow over the rest of his career. Conversely, it seems that everything previous to this film from the brilliant life of Ruth Gordon culminated in 'Maude'. It's an exquisite legacy.

Harold: **I love you Maude.**
Maude: **That's wonderful. Now go love some more.**

▶▶

LEON

Date:	1994
Director:	Luc Besson
Writer(s):	Luc Besson
Runtime(s):	110 minutes (USA), 136 minutes (France)
Country:	France, US
Language:	English

IF YOU WANT THE JOB DONE RIGHT, HIRE A PROFESSIONAL.

Having also made *The Fifth Element* (1997) and *La Femme Nikita* (1991), director Luc Besson is no stranger to action; the man knows how to pour the eye candy. But *Léon* is set apart from other action films, and in fact is elevated to cult status, because it empowers as much as it exhilarates. Its action swirls around a very unconventional, controversial, and surprisingly resonant relationship. This film balances emotion and suspense in equal parts, owing as much to Shakespearian tragedy as it does to *Die Hard* (1988) or *Lethal Weapon* (1987). It has an inspired premise, is well acted and is gorgeously shot.

Savant hit man Léon (Jean Reno) runs his professional and personal life with little – if any – emotion. He shuffles desperately through crowds in an attempt to remain unnoticed, and always sleeps in a seated position with a gun at his side. The character initially appears 'slow', until we see him on a job – where he works with cunning and ruthless efficiency. Léon's world changes when he decides to help Mathilda (Natalie Portman, in her film debut), the 12-year-old girl who lives in the apartment next to him. While she's out picking up groceries,

Mathilda's family is murdered by corrupt DEA agents as retribution for a deal gone bad with her drug-dealing father.

When Mathilda returns, a lookout guards the door to her family's apartment, but she still manages to glimpse the dead bodies inside. Coolly pretending to be a neighbour, she walks by the carnage and proceeds to knock on Léon's door. She has only met Léon once or twice, and one imagines he has no interest in getting involved. Yet after building incredible suspense, he decides to let her in. The rest of the film explores the 'why' of that decision.

The bloodied, beaten Mathilda turns to Léon and asks, 'Is life always this hard or just when you're a kid?' Léon pauses, and his response to her is unusual: instead of merely protecting the girl, he teaches her to fend for herself so that she can take revenge on the man who killed her family. The film's villain creates very little moral conflict for the audience. Opinions vary wildly about Gary Oldman's performance as the film's main baddie, a corrupt DEA agent. He doesn't just chew scenery, he devours it as if he has a dramatic tapeworm.

Thematically reminiscent of the John Cassavetes' classic *Gloria* (1980), *Léon* manages to conjure genuine sympathy for the characters. You care when Mathilda desperately buzzes Léon's room to escape her family's murderers. You care when Mathilda expresses her love for Léon. You care when Léon sends Mathilda to safety, knowing that he'll never see her again. How many action movies can bring you to tears?

Sure Mathilda has a crush on Léon, but that's what 12-year-old girls do: they get crushes on protective figures. Particularly as he saves her life, she is bound to develop a hero-complex towards him. I have spoken to many women who loved this movie. Anyone who seeks to entirely discredit the 'Electra

Complex' will have a hard time refuting the ardent affection this action film has garnered among women. And there is also something amazingly empowering about a 12-year-old female badass, so possessed of burgeoning sexuality but who also remains that calm and collected in the face of death.

I think one of the few advantages of the shorter American and UK versions is that they retain greater subtlety and nuance in the portrayal of the relationship, allowing for more latitude in audience interpretation. Either way, it's telling that an ambiguous relationship creates more controversy than a double-digit body count.

▶▶

THE MAN WHO FELL TO EARTH

Date:	1976
Director:	Nicolas Roeg
Writer(s):	Paul Mayersberg, Walter Tevis (novel)
Runtime(s):	140 minutes
Country:	UK
Language:	English

YOU HAVE TO BELIEVE IT TO SEE IT.

Science fiction for the Glam Rock age, *The Man Who Fell To Earth* – based on a novel by Walter Tevis – is one of the more character-driven and surreal science-fiction films you're likely to see. The Thin White Duke himself, David Bowie, is perfectly cast as an alien disguised as wealthy English businessman Thomas Jerome Newton. After landing in the American southwest, Newton travels to New York City and makes an incredible proposition to Oliver Farnsworth (Buck Henry), a patents lawyer. He wants him to take charge of World Enterprises, a new corporation specialising in electronics. The money for the business venture comes from nine inventions Newton has patented, including one for self-developing film.

It is revealed that Newton has been sent to Earth in an effort to figure out a way to ship water back to his own drought-ridden planet. He attempts to do this by introducing various bits of superior alien technology, patenting them and reinvesting profits into an aerospace company that can build his craft.

Newton becomes fabulously wealthy overnight. The reclusive tycoon/alien retreats to a small town in New Mexico. He sequesters himself away in a motel and watches 12 television sets simultaneously. It turns out that Newton has learnt about humans through television signals he picked up on his planet. Playing before him is a multileveled montage of our civilisation as reflected in old movies, situation comedies, news reports and commercials. He meets Betty Jo (Candy Clark), a maid in a motel. He is attracted to her kind simplicity. She becomes his lover, nurse and housekeeper. She is his only consistent human contact except for Nathan Bryce (Rip Torn), a chemistry professor, hired to work on a fuel carrying system for the spaceship.

Director Nicolas Roeg – *Performance* (1970), *Walkabout* (1971) and *Don't Look Now* (1973) – has developed a distinct cinematic style. In this film, crosscutting a consciously oblique style and intriguing visuals results in a memorable work. *The Man Who Fell To Earth* is post-pop-art science fiction, a combination of strange flashback/hallucinatory montages, ghostly music (composed by Bowie), eerie alien imagery and a full-on Ziggy Stardust era performance by David Bowie. The film certainly was ground breaking; and, surprisingly, Roeg is able to coalesce the psychedelic meets sci-fi ingredients into a pretty entertaining movie. There is one element that feels more than a little out of place though – the multiple and overly pretentious sex scenes.

The film is a visual feast; anyone who has seen a Roeg film will appreciate that he knows how to set up a shot and exploit natural and artificial light for all it's worth. While always praised for his aesthetic prowess, Roeg is often criticised for an inability to assemble a linear scene, meaning his films often feel disjointed and confusing. This however feels intentional; it differentiates his work generally and, in the case of *The Man Who Fell To Earth*, the style reflects the alien's attempts to make sense of his new surroundings, which provokes his gradual addiction to earthly pleasures such as alcohol, sex and television.

The original version of the film came in at 118 minutes and left some gaping holes in the plot. The more coherent 140-minute director's cut will feel a bit more cogent. Even so, the longer version is challenging science fiction. Its scattered narrative might isolate some, but if you enjoy some cerebral sci-fi that takes a stylistic risk or two, then you'll probably be glad you discovered this justified cult classic.

▶▶

MONTY PYTHON AND THE HOLY GRAIL

Date:	1975
Directors:	Terry Gilliam, Terry Jones
Writer(s):	Graham Chapman, John Cleese
	Eric Idle, Terry Gilliam, Terry Jones,
	Michael Palin
Runtime(s):	91 minutes
Country:	UK
Language:	English

SETS THE CINEMA BACK 900 YEARS.

There are two common ways to become familiar with *Monty Python and the Holy Grail.* You might rent the film and view it yourself, or you might somehow find yourself in the company of an under-socialised fan who will recite every line to you. While the experience of the former is sublime, I suggest that slamming your hand in a car door is infinitely preferable to the latter.

Michael Palin, (the late) Graham Chapman, Terry Gilliam, Eric Idle, John Cleese and Terry Jones are all equally wonderful. Never has a subject of parody been attacked with such authority and expertise. The ensemble is split nearly evenly between alumni of Cambridge and Oxford with backgrounds in history or literature (with the exception of Graham Chapman who was a certified medical doctor). Consequently, the most absurd take on the medieval genre may also be one of the most authentic ever produced.

Medieval England was a shit-soaked cesspool, whose brutal

codes of romanticised gallantry were in desperate need of a take down. These British comedians reclaim their own history from Hollywood by defiling its mystique in a grotesque, unpleasant and accurate fashion. Genius.

The jokes in this movie are multi-dimensional and are usually masked by extremely perverse and blunt facades. The knights do not actually ride horses, but only skip along holding an imaginary reign while their squire makes appropriate galloping sound effects with coconut shells. No mere artistic device, the $210,000 budget did not allow for horses. They simply embraced the shortcomings and elevated the absurdity, which represents an altogether different, but no less remarkable, genius.

Like the Arthurian legend itself, the film is episodic, which is a fantastic forum for sketch comedians to move into feature films. The premise is simple: it is a satire of the Arthurian legend where King Arthur bands together the knights of the round table to go on a quest to seek the holy grail. We are therefore introduced to a range of unlikely looking knights who each encounter various obstacles on their quest. We have:

Sir Lancelot the Brave (John Cleese), who mistakes a fey and reluctant groom for a damsel in distress, thereby turning the wedding party of a politically-motivated arranged marriage into a bloodbath;

Sir Robin the Not-Quite-So-Brave-as-Sir Launcelot (Eric Idle), whose minstrels regale him constantly with songs about his lack of exploits, 'Brave Sir Robin who *ran away, he ran away*';

The science-minded Sir Bedevere (Terry Jones), who illustrates the Logic of Witch Burning ('If she weighs the same as a duck, she's made of wood – and therefore ... a witch!');

Sir Galahad the Pure (Michael Palin), who confronts 160

beautiful young women 'all between the ages of 17 and 22' at Castle Anthrax who are starving for male attention and insisting on spankings and oral sex;

Lat but not least, King Arthur himself (Graham Chapman), who encounters politically aware peasants ('I didn't vote for you', 'Help! Help! I'm being repressed!') who take the piss out of the Arthurian legend by declaring: 'Listen, strange women lyin' in ponds distributin' swords is no basis for a system of government!'

Add to this Insulting Frenchmen who are mysteriously in England, the Knights who Until Recently said 'Ni!', a vicious man-eating rabbit, a holy hand grenade, the perilous bridge of death, the *deus ex machina* of animators suffering fatal heart attacks and a black knight who is undeterred by 'a simple flesh wound' (at this point he's losing a limb with each strike).

In addition to each playing a knight, all the performers play multiple roles wonderfully. It is a great piece of ensemble writing and performance but, to me personally, this movie cements John Cleese's much-deserved reputation as the funniest man alive. From his remarkable Sir Lancelot, to his portrayal of a French stereotype in overdrive (of the movable castle), to his shimmering Black Knight ('Come back here!'), Cleese never speaks a line (or makes an appearance) that isn't brilliant.

See it, love it and see it again. And then if you still long for something completely different, check out *Monty Python's Life Of Brian* (1979) and *Monty Python's The Meaning of Life* (1983) to witness the evolution of the group's comedic sensibilities.

▶▶

MY DINNER WITH ANDRE

Date:	1981
Director:	Louis Malle
Writer(s):	André Gregory, Wallace Shawn
Runtime(s):	110 minutes
Country:	US
Language:	English

I ALWAYS ENJOY FINDING OUT ABOUT PEOPLE.
EVEN IF THEY ARE IN ABSOLUTE AGONY,
I ALWAYS FIND IT VERY INTERESTING.

In some ways true conversation can be more intimate than sex. It is no wonder then that the latter is portrayed constantly and the former almost never. However, like sex, conversation is only as interesting as the participants.

My Dinner with André is essentially and entirely a real-time dinner conversation between André Gregory and Wallace Shawn, each playing a simulacrum of their actual selves. Now before you presume anything about a film in which two men continue a dialogue throughout, remember that 'conversation' is a broad experience and can be as vague a term as 'food', ranging from horrid to excellent. This film is several courses of the latter. And like eating, talking has a sensuality of its own.

This film is very self-possessed. It appeals to a small audience not because it failed to hit with a wider one, but because it trusted the one for which it was intended. That audience in turn was very grateful and turned it into a 'word of mouth' hit. All of this movie's alleged 'flaws' (too slow, too talky, too heady) are deliberate. The director, Louis Malle, has built a critique of his characters and himself into the movie. He knows that many people will be turned off, but rewards those who come along.

The film illustrates the strength of oral history as a process of give and take. Just when the views of the characters seem most polarised, they again find common ground. And when one makes a point with which he's sure the other will agree, he sometimes finds that he has lost the complicity of his conversational partner. This mirrors not only conversation, but also human interaction in a broader sense.

The aspirations of this are so grand and so completely satisfied that one both marvels at Shawn and laughs at the role he has chosen for himself. André's experiences are so much of a hallucinogenic/mythical nature that no cinematic image could match those created in our heads. It's effective cinema.

To this extent, it doesn't matter if Wally and André are discussing metaphysics or Wally's electric blanket. While I grant that their topics are, on the whole, only interesting to an audience likely to appreciate this type of film, I think that the subject matter is more a device than crucial plot point. The subjects of the conversation serve to draw the audience into Malle's intent, but what we may learn has little to do with what is being discussed. A movie is an event in itself, regardless of content. There is a communal experience of watching what thousands have watched. Without meaning to, this worthy film exemplifies the tragedy of human communication: that it is elusive and ephemeral.

This film holds up after repeat viewings because so many of the set pieces reach such profound and challenging levels. In fact, you almost have to see it many times over a period of many years to appreciate just how good it is. One of the highlights is when André is talking to Wally about a strange, experimental evening he spent with friends on Long Island one Halloween. His voice conveys pure, authentic personal experience, trembling as he tells the story.

If you find André a little pretentious, by the way, which many people will, don't necessarily believe that this wasn't deliberate. Wally himself finds his friend somewhat pretentious also, yet admits that he doesn't exactly have his life in any order either. In his opening monologue, he complains that all he used to think about was art, but now the only thing he thinks about is money. Wally (and the audience), through his encounter with André, learns to jump-start his life, realising that everything in his life has meaning.

►►

► NETWORK

Date:	1976
Director:	Sidney Lumet
Writer(s):	Paddy Chayefsky
Runtime(s):	120 minutes
Country:	US
Language:	English

TELEVISION WILL NEVER BE THE SAME!
PREPARE YOURSELF FOR A
PERFECTLY OUTRAGEOUS
MOTION PICTURE.

Not only is Paddy Chayefsky's *Network* just as relevant as it was when it was made, it has proven to be downright prophetic. I make a point of viewing this film every two years or so, and each time I do it only seems truer. The state of network news has degenerated to such a level that what was posed as absurd dark comedy in 1975, has actually been exceeded by reality. I suggest that given another five to ten years of decline in media standards, video stores will be required to reclassify *Network* from 'drama' to 'documentary'.

The film opens during a shift in corporate structure of the fictitious UBS television network. This fourth network is struggling for ratings and turns its news division over to the control of its entertainment division. Consequently, Howard Beale (Peter Finch), the aging UBS news anchor, is fired by the network. He reacts by announcing on live television his intention to commit suicide on air. After a media frenzy, the next day he turns what is meant to be his apology into a rant that culminates in insisting that people go to their windows and yell, 'I'm mad as hell, and I'm not going to take it anymore.' Which they do en masse. Beale becomes a major TV sensation and one of the most valuable assets to the parent company, CCA, that is gradually taking control of UBS. As a result he is given his own show as 'the mad prophet of the air-waves'. He appears live on television every weekday evening to tell the real truth to the people of America. The program is a huge success but Beale uses his power to make startling revelations about CCA, leaving its executives with a serious problem.

The film boasts a cache of tour de force performances. William Holden is remarkable as ever as an old guard producer who sees, but is unable to stop, the grotesque decline of news standards. Peter Finch gives an Oscar-winning (sadly posthumously) performance as the anchorman who has been driven to a mental breakdown. Faye Dunaway tags the role of her career as Diana Christensen, the seemingly confident career woman who is coming apart at the seams. Beatrice Straight won an Oscar for her five-and-a-half minute part as Holden's betrayed but forgiving wife. Robert Duvall continued his streak of great films in the 70s as Frank Hackett, the TV station's cold-as-ice hatchet man. And Ned Beatty proves that he is a magnificent actor, receiving an Oscar nomination for a brief but perfectly scripted and perfectly delivered monologue.

When you break the script down you find that, for the most part, *Network* is a series of precise, fine-tuned monologues. And there is nothing wrong with that. While the dialogue is often heavy-handed, it never drifts into didactic sermonising. The film avoids this by virtue of its cast and thir commitment to its point of view. Likewise, lesser actors might have relied on the dialogue alone to propel the film. The cast completely inhabit their roles with complexity and life. So often a project that combines this much talent fails to equal the sum of its parts.

While the number of academy award wins and nominations certify *Network* as a mainstream classic, it is the following it has generated over time that affirms its cult status. Most classic films are viewed as signifiers of the time of their production; as nostalgic period representations of the state of the art. *Network* is the rarest of films in that it grows more resonant with each passing year. Because of its almost eerie prescience, it is actually building momentum with time. No movie since has come close to hitting the subject of media frenzy, America's obsession with television and mass-market sensationalism quite as well as *Network*. It is a film so iconic in the media world, you would think that someone, somewhere in the echelons of power, would consciously try to avoid its prophecy.

▶▶

▶ # PERFORMANCE

Date:	1970
Director(s):	Donald Cammell, Nicolas Roeg
Writer(s):	Donald Cammell
Runtime(s):	105 minutes
Country:	UK
Language:	English

SEE THEM ALL IN A FILM ABOUT FANTASY.
AND REALITY. VICE. AND VERSA.

As Jagger's character says in the movie: 'The only performance
that makes it, that really makes it, that makes it all the way, is
the one that achieves madness!' And *Performance* achieves it.
It's a beautiful little freaky stripy beast, darling.

A petty gangster's flight for his life culminates in something
more frightening still: he discovers in himself so much of what
he loathes in others. James Fox plays Chas, who is on the run
from both the law and the mob. He takes refuge in a Notting
Hill home, which he finds is occupied by reclusive rock star
Turner (Mick Jagger), his junkie girlfriend Pherber (Anita
Pallenberg) and her French lover Lucy (French teen actress
Michèle Breton).

Performance merges the hard-boiled, Cockney gangster world
of the Kray twins exemplified by James Fox's brutal Chas, with
the freaks of the rock/drug world of Jagger's enigmatic Turner.
The film deals with the concepts of duality and personality
exchange. As Turner interacts with Chas, Chas's perception
of reality begins to change (with a little help of some
hallucinogenic drugs) and their lives become intertwined.

Reality and fantasy blur, gender and personas get confused and Chas and Turner become increasingly hard to tell apart as Chas is initiated into Turner's underworld of drug experimentation and gender bending.

Turner's name in itself is symbolic of the way he tries to play with and turn Chas's psyche around. It is ultimately Turner's 'performance' that brings the two worlds together, as he poses as Chas's mobster boss, Harry Flowers, in a scene similar to a contemporary music video. It all leads up to a startling and ambiguous ending.

Performance captures the perverse sub-culture of organised 'working class' gangsters with an unromanticised authenticity. James Fox is cast against type, yet is entirely effective as a violent and merciless mobster with a secret. German/Italian actress Anita Pallenberg is beautiful, decadent, dangerous, high, yet also grounded and very much herself as Pherber. You can see why Keith Richards, Brian Jones, and Mick Jagger all fell for her charms. But the film makes perfect use of Mick Jagger. The movie was shot chronologically and Jagger seems to be growing as an actor in each scene. Witness the 'Memo From Turner' sequence and you'll see my point. It also features some of Mick Jagger's finest musical moments at the peak of his prime – playing blues guitar, singing and dancing in a scene where he regains his 'demon'.

All of this unfolds to an ultra-cool soundtrack of The Last Poets, Randy Newman, Jagger's lost classic 'Memo From Turner' and former Spector/Stones/Crazy Horse collaborator Jack Nitzsche's Moog.

It's a misnomer to give sole credit to Nic Roeg as director. Roeg and Cammell co-directed it. In fact, according to Cammell, they worked so well together that people commented that the two director approach was the wave of the future. Roeg was the Director of Photography, bringing his always stunning camera work to the film, but Donald Cammell wrote, directed the actors, and edited the film (along with Frank Mazzola).

Performance essentially plays reality and non-reality against one another, simultaneously reinforcing and debunking the mythic era of the late 1960s. That said, several decades later, this movie is still ahead of its time. It's a cinematic marvel and metaphysical mindbender. It is in turns glamorous and seedy. Gritty social reality and otherworldly fantasy merge in a conundrum that holds one's emotions as much as one's intellect.

▶▶

PINK FLAMINGOS

Date:	1972
Director:	John Waters
Writer(s):	John Waters
Runtime(s):	93 minutes
Country:	USA
Language:	English

AN EXERCISE IN POOR TASTE.

Though there are several films from Waters' body of work that qualify for cult status, *Pink Flamingos* is the film against which all others are ultimately judged. It is his first feature, one of the more infamous works of celluloid and a genuine cinematic Rorschach test.

Legendary drag queen Divine (Glenn Milstead) lives in a trailer with her retarded mother Edie (Edith Massey), chicken-loving son Crackers (Danny Mills) and 'travelling companion' Cotton (Mary Vivian Pearce). Divine has recently been featured in a tabloid as the 'Filthiest Person in the World', and she wants to keep that title.

Connie and Raymond Marble (Mink Stole and David Lochary), an odd, haute couture white trash couple – if you can imagine such a thing – are incensed at Divine's publicity. They consider themselves the filthiest people alive as evidenced by, among other things, cruising the streets for female hitchers who they abduct, hold in their basement and force their hapless butler Channing (Channing Wilroy) to impregnate. It's all part of an illegal adoption ring, selling babies to lesbian couples to fund an inner-city grade school heroin ring and a string of pornography shops. Still interested?

In an hour and a half the we get artificial insemination, an incestuous blowjob, toe-sucking fetishism, a naked man lifting his legs over his head so the camera may zoom in on his asshole as it dilates to the strains of 'Surfin' Bird', a rape scene in which a live chicken is bloodied and killed, and the legendary 'dog shit eating scene'. How about now?

The tagline 'An exercise in poor taste' is certainly an understatement. *Pink Flamingos* involves graphic depictions of almost every kind of depravity imaginable. And therein lies the integrity of the film: if you set out to shock, why not go all the way?

The depictions of perversion in this film are remarkable for the lack of self-consciousness from the characters themselves. There appears to be no judgment or repulsion within the film. The entire universe of *Pink Flamingos* makes perfect sense to its participants.

Waters never gives up the philosophic core by which his work would soon become noted: spotlighting the most repellent, bottom-grade ideals and portraying them as normal, almost subdued. It's clear the 'perverts' have gotten hold of the means of production, hence the ease with which the participants push boundaries. They are not boundaries to them, and in no way do they seem to share or even anticipate the value system of the observers. Most films that portray any kind of deviance usually do so consciously to shock or titillate. In *Pink Flamingos*, these occurrences simply are.

John Waters had at his disposal people who would willingly do the things the script asked of them. In Waters' logic, why not do them? It seems everyone enjoyed making the film, and this sense of joy is infectious. It lets the viewer off the hook from the concern that anyone is exploited, which is itself a sensation stranger than shock.

The twenty-fifth anniversary reissue includes several previously edited scenes (the film had editing?) and commentary at the end in which Waters' addresses some of the audience reaction to the film. Most noteworthy is his response to the scene in which a chicken is crushed to death during a rape: 'I eat chicken, and as far as I know, the chicken on my plate didn't get there from a heart attack. Hey, it died on camera and it got to fuck.' Dismissive? Maybe. But the logic indicts the practices of the off-camera world, and doesn't hold the film's portrayal to any higher standard.

The most gratuitous scene involves a live poodle defecating on a sidewalk, after which Divine happily devours it. Even more gratuitous is that this scene comes after the climax and resolution of the 'plot'. There is no reason for this scene, except as a last resort to make sure everyone is offended before they leave the cinema, and to make sure they leave talking about it.

Before you view *Pink Flamingos* be warned and remember what John Waters said: 'I take pride in the fact that my work has no socially redeeming value. But always remember that there is good bad taste and bad bad taste.'

▶▶

PINK FLOYD – THE WALL

Date:	1982
Director:	Alan Parker
Writer(s):	Roger Waters (also album The Wall)
Runtime(s):	95 minutes
Country:	UK
Language:	English

THE MEMORIES. THE MADNESS. THE MUSIC... THE MOVIE.

Pink Floyd – The Wall has occasionally been categorised as 'a stoner film', implying that the experience is somehow enhanced under the influence. However, I must disagree; this is not a motion picture of slow and trippy images, it is a true attack on the senses that might leave a viewer depressed or shocked, and I have the impression that under the influence of drugs the experience could be unsettling. Nor is it a movie for the clinically depressed. This movie is brutally harsh and makes virtually no attempt to tell the viewers things don't always go this bad in life. In fact, it seems to go out of its way to drill into your head just how horrible life is. In short, apply the same caution in watching this film as you would to operating heavy machinery.

The rock opera and the rock opus were a stark contrast to previous incarnations of rock 'n' roll, which emphasised individuality, freedom and fun. If it had all been a party up to this point, then *Pink Floyd – The Wall* represents the hangover. It's a vision of the 1980s from the perspective of the sobering adolescents of the 1960s, the legacy of a 1950s childhood, and the post-WWII let down. It demystifies youth, celebrity and exploration as a starting ground. It reads as psychological drama; it's very personal and very raw.

Alan Parker and Roger Waters made an audacious and seductive film, but the music is truly the star, helping to evoke some pretty powerful images. If you are not a fan of the album, there is really no point in watching. Each sequence of the film mirrors songs of the double-album (the associations of which I have delineated with parentheses below). The result is a compelling story that peers into the mind of an overprotected, reclusive and sometimes-violent rock star named Pink (played as a child by Kevin McKeon and as an adult by singer Bob Geldof). Events that lead up to his mental breakdown are depicted through confused, random and fairly hallucinogenic memories.

As a child, Pink lost his father in WWII ('Another Brick in the Wall, Part 1' and especially the heartbreaking sequence of 'When The Tigers Broke Free') and was raised by an overprotective mother ('Mother'). In school, his teachers denied him the possibility of expressing his own creativity ('The Happiest Days of Our Lives', 'Another Brick in the Wall, Part 2'). Growing older, Pink starts playing in a rock band which brings him popularity; but popularity and money work only on a superficial level, and for his inability to cope with his own past and frustrations he seeks refuge in drugs. Mind-altering drugs only accelerate his mental detachment from the outside world, and when he discovers that his wife is cheating on him ('Empty Spaces') – not that much of a surprise, since Pink is by now quite disturbed and not paying much attention to her – he puts 'the final pieces' into a mental 'wall' he's allowed his own mind to build as an escape from the real world ('Another Brick in the Wall, Part 3', 'Goodbye Cruel World'). However, when the wall is built, Pink realises that he is not able to come back to reality, no matter how hard he tries ('Is There Anybody Out There?'). Desperate and angered, Pink fantasises of becoming a loathsome dictator to inflict punishment on the outside world that did wrong to him ('In the Flesh', 'Run Like Hell', 'Waiting for the Worms'). At this point, all the borders between reality and psychosis are confused, and we don't know how much his fantasies are a distorted vision of reality: the Nazi-looking followers could be fans at a concert who are foolishly following his orders and seeing him as a godlike figure, or maybe he just thinks they are. Then again, it could be that the whole thing is in his mind.

Repulsed by the pathetic and repulsive figure he has become, Pink turns all the blame on to himself ('Trial') and sentences himself as 'guilty' for all that happened to him. The film ends in a way that can lead to multiple interpretations, as we don't know whether Pink really gets free from the chains of insanity. However, there is a strong and touching hint of hope.

You will be hard pressed to find a film that takes such a deep, relentless ride within a character's psyche as *Pink Floyd – The Wall.* Proving that dialogue is all but unnecessary, this film takes you deeper into the character's mind than perhaps you'd want to go. Much of this is autobiographical material combining the experiences of two members of the original band: Syd Barrett and Roger Waters. Syd Barrett, the former leader and creative mind behind Pink Floyd, fell into schizophrenia and to this day lives in seclusion.

Most of the film is shot in the style of a music video and, for once in cinema, that is a good thing. There is very little dialogue, but a story is still told by Water's melancholy songs and Gerald Scarfe's amazing and potent animation. While it sometimes feels as though the movie is pieced together like a hammered jigsaw puzzle, some of the set pieces are just too good to allow the structure to ruin the overall experience. There are some intense and violent metaphors in both the animation and live action sequences that illustrate not only personal illnesses, but social ones as well.

As can be expected, this film also relies heavily on the use of walls as symbolism, and they can range from blatantly obvious to severely subtle. The album contrasts themes of peace and violence, and has a cyclical set-up. The movie does much of the same, in that it examines the cycles of hatred, power and rejuvenation. A fine example of this is the teacher who is abused at home by his 'fat and psychopathic wife' and then takes his powerlessness away by exercising power over the pupils, one of whom (Pink) grows up to envision himself exercising his own power over the weak.

I would say the Orwellian themes are now less resonant. We probably have more to fear from bland, happy mindlessness than any oppressive government agency. And if there is one overwhelming drawback to the film, unrelated to moviemaking, it's that some of the imagery in the film may eclipse your own conception of the music.

All in all, this film is a must-see for Pink Floyd fans, fans of poetry, fans of cult films, fans of avant-garde movies or just a casual moviegoer with an hour and a half to kill and money to spare. If you are renting/buying do yourself a favour and see it in widescreen. The film is too claustrophobic in pan and scan; and you miss the full effects of the presentation, particularly the animation.

▶▶

▸ PLAN 9 FROM OUTER SPACE

Date:	1959
Director:	Ed Wood Jr.
Writer(s):	Ed Wood Jr.
Runtime(s):	79 minutes
Country:	US
Language:	English

UNSPEAKABLE HORRORS FROM OUTER SPACE PARALYSE THE LIVING AND RESURRECT THE DEAD!

Often referred to as the 'the worst film ever made', *Plan 9 from Outer Space* is also an exceedingly popular cult favourite. The easiest explanation for this affection is the last word – 'made'. A film like this deserves credit for existing at all and I think that is part of *Plan 9*'s enduring appeal.

There are mediums where artists can remain solitary and mad in their genius (painters etc), but film is a collective venture. How charismatic and driven does a person have to be to pull an entire production chain together? Now imagine someone with an abysmal body of work doing it with an idea this bad, and assembling a cast that managed to act as unimaginatively as the material merits. Ed Wood married vision to delusion like no director before or since. He is so studiously, hysterically bad.

Anyway, the plot involves a superior alien culture concerned that humanity is advancing to such a degree as to threaten the stability of the universe. They arrive on Earth and institute 'Plan 9' (one wonders what plans 1-8 were), which involves raising the dead from their graves, and sending them on a plodding rampage. The army and the cops try to stop an invasion consisting of three dead people ... walking ... very slowly.

The cheapness of the production and the obvious continuity errors vie for notoriety: cockpits consisting only of cardboard and a shower curtain, gravestones that blow over, inexplicable sudden changes between night and day and pointless stock footage from war propaganda films. One of the best bits occurs when a police officer uses the end of his revolver's barrel to scratch his head in puzzlement. The most legendary miscalculation of course involves horror icon Bela Lugosi, who died early in the production. Rather than reshoot the sequences with Lugosi's character, Ed Wood mixed footage of Lugosi with footage using his replacement (Ed Wood's chiropractor), who was nearly a foot taller then Lugosi.

Maybe you think the film might have sounded good on paper, and was simply a production misfire. You'd be both generous and wrong. Inane dialogue has never been spoken with more Shakespearian earnestness. From the start there is Criswell's opening narration: 'Greetings my friends. We are all interested in the future. For that is where you and I are going to spend the rest of our lives. And remember, my friends, future events such as these will affect you in the future.' Then there is the classic: 'One thing's sure. Inspector Clay's dead. Murdered. And someone's responsible'. And do not forget the Harold Pinter worthy: 'I saw a flying saucer.' – 'Saucer? You mean the kind from up there?' – 'Yeah, or its counterpart'. Or the Aristotelian deduction in 'Visits? But that would mean visitors!'

The film's pleasures aren't limited to the Schadenfreude of bad writing and bad continuity. There are also a few moments of entirely accidental genius. The film radically supposes that earthlings are at best dangerously naive and a threat to other more intelligent beings. Not many films have ever been made with human arrogance as the villain, especially not in the 50s. And so, the alien berates the humans with classic Ed Wood dialogue: 'Your stupid minds! Stupid! Stupid!' The human responds by punching him in the jaw. Irony – pure, sublime and entirely accidental.

The Tim Burton bio-pic about Ed Wood Jr. has been a blessing and a curse. It raises expectations for how bad *Plan 9* will be, and yet it also diminishes the mystique by conjecturing answers to 'What were they thinking?' If you want to hear the answer from the stars, backers and friends of Ed Wood, pick up the Ed Wood Jr. biography *Nightmare of Ecstasy*. The film *Ed Wood* (1994) is loosely based on it.

To be honest, *Plan 9* isn't even Ed Wood's worst. See *Glen or Glenda* (1953), *Bride of the Monster* (1955), *Night of the Ghouls* (1959) or *Orgy of the Dead* (1965) before you judge *Plan 9*. And let's not be hasty to declare Ed Wood the worst filmmaker either, lest we forget that Michael Bay isn't done yet.

▶▶

THE PRINCESS BRIDE

Date:	1987
Director:	Rob Reiner
Writer(s):	William Goldman (book and screenplay)
Runtime(s):	98 minutes
Country:	USA
Language:	English

SCALING THE CLIFFS OF INSANITY,
BATTLING RODENTS OF UNUSUAL SIZE,
FACING TORTURE IN THE PIT OF DESPAIR —
TRUE LOVE HAS NEVER BEEN A SNAP.

Rob Reiner crafts a great movie here: whether you have kids or whether you're an auteur, I dare you not to love this movie. *The Princess Bride* was that movie that you *really* wanted to see, and yet you didn't for a host of incredibly stupid reasons. It boasts a caring, touching and beautifully hip script by *Butch Cassidy and The Sundance Kid* (1969) author William Goldman. *The Princess Bride* still stands as an effective comedy, an interesting bedtime tale, and one of the greatest date rentals of all time.

   The Princess Bride is an enchanting film about 'fencing, fighting, torture, revenge, giants, monsters, chases, escapes, true love, miracles' and more. Based on William Goldman's equally entertaining novel (which was inspired, he says, when he asked his then-young daughters what he should write about and one said 'a princess,' and the other said 'a bride'). The humour isn't so much over-the-top or silly as much as it is street-wise with a modern consciousness. The characters aren't so much relics of the past as much as they are contemporary stowaways in a touching but goofy old-fashioned fairy tale.

Beautiful Buttercup (Robin Wright, before she added 'Penn' to her name) falls for handsome, sweet, farm-boy Westley (Cary Elwes), only to learn that he's been killed by pirates while out seeking his fortune. Grief-stricken, she agrees to marry pompous Prince Humperdinck (Chris Sarandon), but is kidnapped by a trio of unsavoury types – Napoleonic Sicilian Vizzini (Wallace Shawn), fiery Spanish swordsman Inigo Montoya (Mandy Patinkin) and gentle giant Fezzik (André the Giant). After she's rescued from their clutches by a mysterious man in black, Buttercup begins to realise her Westley may not be quite so dead after all. But since we all know that the course of true love never does run smooth, the pair has to face a few more obstacles (fire swamps, death machines, six-fingered men - you know, the usual dating roadblocks) before they can be together. Cameos from the likes of Billy Crystal (Miracle Max), Carol Kane (Valerie) and Peter Cook (the Impressive Clergyman) round off the impressive cast on the fairy-tale end of things, while Peter Falk and Fred Savage offer a nice framework for the film as the grandfather sharing the story with his sick grandson.

The actors are all first-rate – Wright nails her English accent, and Elwes is the perfect Douglas Fairbanks-meets-Errol Flynn swashbuckling hero – and Goldman gives them a sharp, funny script to work with. Director Reiner has said that *The Princess Bride* is one of the movies people most often quote back to him, and it's not hard to see why. It has several memorable lines: 'Hello. My name is Inigo Montoya. You killed my father. Prepare to die,' and 'Bye, bye, boys! Have fun storming the castle!' this is one awfully quotable flick. In fact, with its unique combination of anachronistic humour and sigh-inducing romance, it's next to impossible to figure out why *The Princess Bride* only did so-so in cinemas, finally taking off when it was released on video.

I was pretty convinced at one time that Cary Elwes was in the perfect position to become the next Errol Flynn. He's almost as suave, daring and impressive as Harrison Ford's Indiana Jones. His Westley out-duels a fencing expert, takes down a giant, out-wits a genius and returns from being 'mostly dead' all in the utmost dashing fashion. Mandy Patinkin's Inigo Montoya readily recognises that he has wasted his entire life searching to avenge his father's death. He admits hilariously that there seems to be little money in the revenge business, and his eventual disposal of Christopher Guest (Count Tyrone Rugen) is perhaps the most heartfelt, touching and gratifying murder ever filmed. Chances are after watching it that you'll be happier than a hippie the day Richard Nixon resigned. Long live the dread pirate Roberts, whoever he is these days!

▶▶

QUADROPHENIA

Date:	1979
Director:	Franc Roddam
Writer(s):	Dave Humphries, Franc Roddam, Martin Stellman and Pete Townshend
Runtime(s):	120 minutes
Country:	UK
Language:	English

A WAY OF LIFE.

Quadrophenia has directorial flair, an excellent soundtrack and some underrated scripting and performances. It perfectly captures the angst and disillusionment of its protagonist.

Inspired by The Who's 1973 source album, Roddam's film immerses viewers in the action, relegating The Who's music largely to the background, achieving an almost vérité feel. The film is not a marketing vehicle or homage, but rather a companion piece to the album. Many songs are conspicuously absent, while some great songs from Booker T. and the MG's to Motown's finest are included. And that's okay; it would almost be redundant for 'Cut Your Hair' to play in a film that already expresses its spirit so well. It is a testament to Roddam that the source album is a thematic and emotional point of reference, sparing *Quadrophenia* from becoming a 'mime along'. It's a reverse of Ken Russell's *Tommy* (1975); which may have been a better album, but was an abysmal film.

It's London, 1965, and a young man wants to rise above the monotony of his working class existence: Jimmy (Phil Daniels) is a pill-addicted young lad in a dead-end job. He tells his cynical friend Kevin (Ray Winstone), 'You have to be *something* don't you, otherwise you might as well jump in the sea and drown – that's why I'm a Mod, see!' Daniels' character is a volatile adolescent mix of arrogance and fear, which play out in equal measure with few outlets to relieve either. Being part of a pack, 'The Mods', provides some comfort, and the joys and limitations of that experience form the boundaries of the film. The affiliation affords him sex, drugs and violence, but none seem to satisfy. When all his friends have found female companions at a wild party, Jimmy is reduced to smashing up the garden with his scooter to relieve his frustration. When all the girls in the ballroom are admiring the 'Ace Face' (Sting), Jimmy takes a potentially fatal dive off the balcony and into the crowd below.

It is almost painful to see Jimmy go through the highs of his weekend in Brighton, and the subsequent comedown to the dreariness of everyday life. You can feel his emotion when he realises the truth about Sting's character ('Bellboy!'). The final half-hour is absolutely riveting as Jimmy finally falls apart.

Following Jimmy's rounds from clubs to parties to record shops, and back to his memento-adorned room, *Quadrophenia* acts as a time machine, recreating a stretch of the 60s when Mods championed English bands (particularly The Who), trolled London streets on Vespa scooters and challenged their leather-sporting rivals, the Rockers.

In 1979 when this film was released, mod fashion was undergoing a resurgance. And some of the actors – Ray Winstone, Michael Elphick, and Leslie Ash, to name a few – have become household names in the UK. The strange thing is that lead actor Phil Daniels has never since been cast in anything worthy of the substantial talent he displayed here.

Any continuity errors reflect a wonderful thematic transcendence of time, and perhaps even an inside joke. Look for a couple of anachronisms like the double reissue of The Who's *A Quick One/ Sell Out* in the party scene, long before either album was even recorded. There are dozens of bad films that are overly detailed love affairs with retro props, but are tone deaf to authentic characterisation. This film declares itself dead-on to the mood and nuances of everyday life. Those subtleties make it a timeless classic.

▶▶

RE-ANIMATOR

Date:	1985
Director:	Stuart Gordon
Writer(s):	Stuart Gordon, H.P. Lovecraft (book),
	William Norris III, Dennis Paoli
Runtime(s):	86 minutes, 95 min (USA, unrated version)
Country:	USA
Language:	English

HERBERT WEST HAS A VERY GOOD HEAD ON
HIS SHOULDERS ... AND ANOTHER ONE
IN A DISH ON HIS DESK.

Occasionally a low budget film will have the audacity to invoke a high concept and deliver upon it despite financial restrictions. Made in 1985 with a budget of less than $1 million, *Re-Animator* still manages to be one of the most visually rich horror films of the 1980s. Director Stuart Gordon reached new heights of inspired gore in a witty and well-paced tale of an unstable researcher who has discovered a way of re-animating dead tissue.

Based on the H.P. Lovecraft short-story collection *Herbert West: Re-Animator*, the film combines all of the stories into one film. Jeffrey Combs as the title character is a creepy yet strangely likeable medical student who's invented a serum that brings the dead back to life ... sort of. He transfers from a medical school 'somewhere in Switzerland' to the fictitious Miskatonic University, supposedly in the USA. Unfortunately, West's headstrong opinions clash with those of eminent Medical School Professor Dr. Hill (David Gale). West is expelled and forced to continue his experiments in his basement.

Dr. West's housemate Dr. Dan Cain (Bruce Abbott) is West's worried straight man. At first Cain is shocked by the experiments, but his curiosity slowly compels him to cooperate with West. Dan's fiancée Megan (Barbara Crampton) is, in keeping with horror film convention, beautiful and, for convenience of plot, also the Dean's daughter.

As West's behaviour becomes more irresponsible, his experiments veer out of control. The re-animations escalate into chaos and Dan realises he's in over his head. Soon erstwhile corpses develop minds of their own, leading to a head-on clash between re-animated and re-animators.

When attempting a horror-comedy hybrid, it is very easy to slip too far in either direction, but this movie mixes the grotesque with humour perfectly. The two genres intersect most blatantly when both the slang term and a literal interpretation of 'giving head' fuse in a now legendary scene.

Roger Ebert once said this film 'has the courage of its lack of convictions'. *Re-Animator* finds humour in lurid excess. These people cared about the tone and the effect of this material, therefore they acted upon it fearlessly. This audacious slant on the horror genre succeeds mainly through its brisk pacing, wonderfully over-the-top script, and committed performances, especially from the intense Combs.

Every bit of gore was conceived, engineered and executed through the craftsmanship of make-up artist Anthony Doublin and FX creator John Naulin. Their special effects are even more impressively macabre, considering the low budget and that the film was made in the pre-CGI era. They managed to create severed heads, flying intestines and other body parts, murderous naked cadavers and some interesting dissection scenes (think Damian Hurst without the smugness).

The scientific conversations don't throw lingo around without respect for the audience's intelligence; they flow logically, in a manner we can follow, while delivering on the level of junk science bluffing.

There are some rather memorable clips of dialogue: 'Cat dead-details later'. 'I had to kill him.' 'You mean he's dead?' 'Not any more'. And even though the morgue set more resembled an over-sized walk-in cooler, the use of scientific lingo seems credible. The concept of re-animation itself never seems implausible, even if the effects aren't always realistic.

The non-rated version is approximately the same length as the R-rated version, which means each version is missing footage. The non-rated version has more gore; whereas the R-rated version retains certain plot elements and exposition. While I have stated that I like and respect the storyline of *Re-Animator*, I have to recommend the non-rated version because, let's be honest, you aren't renting this one for storyline.

Also if you want to see another example of a successful H.P. Lovecraft screen adaptation, check out *From Beyond* (1986) made by the same team.

▶▶

REPO MAN

Date:	1984
Director:	Alex Cox
Writer(s):	Alex Cox
Runtime(s):	92 minutes
Country:	US
Language:	English

... IT'S 4 AM,
DO YOU KNOW WHERE YOUR CAR IS?

Around the time *Repo Man* was released on video it seemed that video might just democratize Indy cinema instead of killing it. Video stores and, in the US, cable television allowed those outside the cultural centres (I was one) access to films otherwise dependant on Indy-friendly cinemas for showing. Couple that with punk disaffection – nothing to do and no money to do it with – and thus watching *Repo Man* became the perfect default for a weekend night.

Along with Dead Kennedy's albums and a few cult novels, *Repo Man* is a gleaming artefact affirming that the Reagan era did not pass by without indictment in its own time. The 1980s were a decade that no one seemed particularly enthused about, even in the mainstream. A time when Emilio Estevez was not synonymous with B-movie over-exposure, but was instead a new face. Most generations have to wait ten years to know their decade was crap, but call it the speed of information, post-modernism or whatever, but many were self-aware in the 80s and *Repo Man* declared it.

Having lost his girlfriend and his menial supermarket job,

punk rocker Otto (Emilio Estevez) meets a guy named Bud (Harry Dean Stanton) who offers him $25 to drive his wife's car out of a 'bad area'. When a handful of angry people start chasing Otto, he realises that something is up, and he discovers that Bud repossesses cars for a living.

When they arrive at the lot, Otto declares 'I ain't gonna be no stinking repo man.' The secretary Marlene hands Otto some cash: 'Too late kid, you already are.' After Otto pours a beer on the floor of the office, Bud hires Otto on the spot. Later another repo man enters the room and wonders who pissed on the floor 'again'.

When an anonymous source posts a $20,000 reward for a missing 1964 Chevy Malibu, it turns out that what's valuable isn't the car itself, but what's in the trunk – which is very hot, glows brightly and kills anyone who comes in contact with it.

It is a movie that only rewards with repeat viewing. The film has the overall flat look of a made-for-TV movie. Characters fade in and out and have no real definition. Events are never clearly explained and certain sequences seem to have no narrative purpose of any sort.

Estevez does a fair enough job in the lead role, but it is the supporting players that deliver the cult calibre performances. Notable is Tracy Walter as the acid-affected mechanic 'Miller'. His John Wayne discussion is brilliant, as well as the line 'Sometimes people just explode'. And Harry Dean Stanton in the role of Bud is a rich, hilarious performance. Alex Cox had intended the role for Dennis Hopper, but in one of those glorious circumstances of second choices Stanton played Bud. I have nothing to say about Harry Dean Stanton that wasn't expressed in the Pop Will Eat Itself song about the actor.

Bud:	You ain't no communist are you?
Otto:	Hell no!
Bud:	That's good. I don't let no communists ride in my car. No Christians either.

Repo Man is packed with more incongruous sight gags than anyone can absorb in one viewing: keep your eyes peeled for the air fresheners, the generic newspaper box and the watches without hands. In Iggy Pop's classic opening title track, there is a line – 'looking for the joke with a microscope' – that alerts the audience to these details. One such gem involves The Circle Jerks doing a lounge version of their song 'When the Shit Hits the Fan', to which Otto mutters 'And I used to like these guys.'

Many of the characters are named after well-known brands of beer: Miller, Bud, Lite, yet the consumer products in the film are not just generic, they are literal. When one character says to another, 'Let's get a drink,' the next shot reveals a close-up of a six-pack labelled 'Drink' being set down next to a convenience store cash register. At one point, Otto eats directly from a generic can labelled 'Food'.

It's a refreshing that this is one of the few films set in Hollywood that makes no reference to the film industry. It's telling of the wider relationship between this Indy classic and mainstream cinema. Alex Cox's film became a major cult item once it began making the art-house rounds a year after its release (an initial run in a string of Southern grind houses and drive-ins, where it was billed as 'an action film', was a resounding failure).

See it, rent it, buy it and tell your friends, 'J. Frank Parnell sent you.'

▶▶

RESERVOIR DOGS

Date:	1992
Director:	Quentin Tarantino
Writer(s):	Quentin Tarantino, Roger Avary
Runtime(s):	99 minutes
Country:	USA
Language:	English

FIVE TOTAL STRANGERS TEAM UP FOR THE
PERFECT CRIME. THEY DON'T KNOW
EACH OTHER'S NAME.
BUT THEY'VE GOT EACH OTHER'S NUMBER.

A great film in its own right and the inspiration for countless bad ones; such is the burden of creating a seminal work. That and having your name turned into an adjective: 'Tarrantinoesque'.

The film uses elements of other great movies, owing a great deal to Stanley Kubrick's *The Killing* (1956) in particular. *Reservoir Dogs* reworks these elements artfully enough to be considered homage and not derivative.

An experienced crime boss and his son hire six thieves to pull off a robbery of a diamond wholesaler. None of the men know each other, and they are assigned code names: Mr. White (Harvey Keitel), Mr. Orange (Tim Roth), Mr. Pink (Steve Buscemi), Mr. Blonde (Michael Madsen) and Nice Guy Eddie (Chris Penn). Thus, if one gets caught, he can't rat out any of the others. Unfortunately, things don't go as planned. One of the 'crooks' is actually an undercover cop. The men walk into a police ambush and, after a bloody shootout, they scatter to escape.

The survivors rendezvous at an assigned location to contemplate their next move and begin dissecting clues as to which of the men was the rat.

It is a masterpiece of structure, artfully using digressive storytelling while sustaining momentum, continuity and style to effective climax. The use of the single location is reminiscent of theatre staging. The recounting of the botched robbery does not come off as expositional, since a large part of the tension comes not from action, but through the perceptions and recriminations of the survivors.

The film recognises that the 'Who is the mole?' story line can only be sustained so long. Thus, once it is revealed, there is a nice series of flashback sequences involving the cop preparing himself for the assignment and ingratiating himself into the confidence of the group.

The performances are top-notch. Steve Buscemi is wonderfully creepy and manic as Mr. Pink. It's also a pleasure to see veteran character actor Laurence Tierney on the screen again as Joe Tabot. Michael Madsen delivers one BadMoFo performance as Mr. Blonde, a devil-may-care sociopath. After watching his most graphic scene, you will never be able to listen to 'Stuck in the Middle With You' in the same way again.

It is Harvey Keitel and Tim Roth who give the film its most touching edge. The relationship between Keitel and Roth has a transcendent element – the bosses may have protected against betrayal, but not loyalty. White develops a very paternal relationship to the mortally-wounded Mr. Orange, creating a trust and honour to protect him at any cost that is challenged in the film's climax.

Ironically, it is Tarrantino himself who gives the least compelling performance. His character is less prominent. If giving a flatter performance was a choice in the service of the ensemble, then it's a testament to his skill as a director.

As much as there are plot twists and clever dialogue, it remains a surprisingly strong character-driven film. The tension builds, and the energy heightens organically. I will not spoil the movie for you, but if you have ever wondered the true meaning behind Madonna's 'Like a Virgin' (and who hasn't?) you will love the opening. And if you love a good Mexican stand-off (and who doesn't?) you will love the climax.

This film was selected over *Pulp Fiction* (1994) because this was the film whose momentum made *Pulp Fiction* so highly anticipated. *Reservoir Dogs* established the precedent by surprising the audience with its very artful style. It was a very small movie ($1.2 million budget) that achieved cult status on the strength of solid reviews and word of mouth. Had there been no *Pulp Fiction*, had Tarrantino been a one trick pony, *Reservoir Dogs* would still have a following.

▶▶

RIVER'S EDGE

Date:	1987
Director:	Tim Hunter
Writer(s):	Neal Jimenez
Runtime(s):	99 minutes
Country:	USA
Language:	English

THE MOST CONTROVERSIAL FILM YOU WILL SEE THIS YEAR.

A gripping study of teen ambivalence with an utter lack of angst, *River's Edge* is a creepy, powerful and under-seen picture featuring clever yet believable dialogue and virtuoso performances. It is an obvious precursor to *Twin Peaks* (the 1990 TV series or the later film *Twin Peaks: Fire Come Walk With Me*, from 1992) in both its theme and its numb overcast atmosphere.

Taking place in a small, nameless, northern Californian town, it follows a group of teenage characters over several days, after one of their friends admits to murdering his girlfriend. The murderer is Samson (Daniel Roebuck), a tall lug of a teen who isn't panicked or remorseful; rather, he is detached and ambivalent. When he tells his friends about it, he doesn't brag. Calmly answering the question 'Where's Jamie?', he responds matter-of-factly 'I killed her'.

There is nothing new about the depiction of violence in movies, nor the presentation of violent youth. But what has changed in this film is the wider sociological context of that violence. The most unsettling shift may be that killers once portrayed as loners, solitary figures driven by their own rage, now commit acts of violence with sombre calculation and accomplices. It's no longer just the acts of violence that disturb, but also the complicity and indifference of others.

River's Edge deals with the ripple effects of violence. It explores how those around the perpetrator are not equipped to process a response. There is no strong reaction, and that may be the new source of dramatic tension; that the collective moral compass is so far off-kilter and that indifference is too pervasive to recognise and prevent someone crossing the line of violence. It's not simply that children can kill children, but that children can kill children and other children do nothing. Not just do nothing to prevent it, but simply feel nothing and do nothing in its wake.

The screenplay written by Neal Jimenez, is loosely based on an actual event that took place in Milpitas, California in 1981. *River's Edge* is laced with black humour which is the source of much of its cult appeal. Although strung together as a taut, sometimes suspenseful narrative, there is no tension or ambiguity surrounding the actual murder. Nor is the murderer himself the most interesting or even central character. *River's Edge* is first and foremost a character study. Jimenez creates multifaceted personalities for his stoner characters, which keeps them from degrading into one-dimension.

The unofficial leader is Layne (Crispin Glover), a wild-eyed, speed-freak who decides the murder is a test of the group's loyalty. Summoning every ounce of twisted logic he can muster and invoking characters from his steady diet of television and movies ranging from Chuck Norris to Starsky and Hutch, he argues that it is the group's duty to protect Samson and cover up the murder. At first Crispin Glover seems to be giving a bad performance until you realise that it is, in fact, Layne who is bad actor in his self-appointed role of group saviour. He is fanatical and determined, even though he has no idea of what to do, and he believes that helping his friend entitles him to beer. When he gets his beer, he then laments his help 'should at least have rated a Michelob'. He then whines, more upset than at the killing itself, that 'It's warm even!' He's not amoral, just weirdly misdirected, dedicated to a moral code that places loyalty to friends above all other considerations.

The group's conscience is Matt (a not-yet-famous Keanu Reeves), a sullen teen who is immediately disgusted by the murder and Layne's desire to cover it up. Matt is the only teen whose family is portrayed substantially. It explains his apparently contradictory nature. Although he is just as much of an alienated juvenile delinquent as Layne and the others, Matt genuinely appears to have some sense of ethical obligation. He cares for his little sister, and even though he clashes with his mother, a single nurse with a live-in boyfriend, it doesn't stop him from caring for her as well.

Dennis Hopper does his signature Dennis-Hopper-eccentric-character-thing as an ex-biker named Feck, a paranoid recluse who clutches at a plastic sex doll. As the dope supplier to the teens, Feck is their only possible adult confidant. Unfortunately he is of little help, claiming to have once loved a woman so much he was forced to kill her.

While the majority of the teen characters in *River's Edge* are asocial and lost, cut off from feelings of responsibility and respect for authority and drifting along the banal currents of drug abuse and petty criminality, Matt's 12-year-old brother, Tim (Joshua John Miller), is actively monstrous. His amorality seems more sinister because he is starting so young. He's aggressive, violent and cruel to the point that even Matt is repulsed by him. Tim skulks along the edges of the narrative, reminding us that no child is too young to embody the worst.

Even in post-Columbine America, where it has become a tragic regularity to hear of children and teenagers committing acts of violence, *River's Edge*, Tim Hunter's 1987 study of youthful alienation in the Reagan era, still disturbs.

▶▶

ROCK 'N' ROLL HIGH SCHOOL

Date:	1979
Director:	Allan Arkush, Joe Dante (uncredited), Jerry Zucker (uncredited)
Writer(s):	Richard Whitley (screenplay), Russ Dvonch (screenplay), Joseph McBride (screenplay), Allan Arkush (story), Joe Dante (story)
Runtime(s):	93 minutes
Country:	US
Language:	English

I WANNA BE SEDATED.

If you are a cult films fan, you are probably more than aware of the Ramones, the seminal New York City punk rock pioneers of the 1970s. *Rock 'n' Roll High School* is almost entirely a vehicle for the Ramones, and has steadily retained cult film status on that basis alone for over 20 years. After the untimely deaths of both Joey Ramone (cancer) in April 2001 and Dee-Dee Ramone (overdose) in June 2002, the film has enjoyed a resurgence of popularity. It has also benefited from the early-80s punk nostalgia that both fashion and popular music are experiencing as I write this.

The late 1970s were one of the more permissive periods in popular culture: a time when parents were as likely to be stoned as the kids, and rock 'n' roll had long been a multi-billion dollar establishment industry. And so an anti-authority film for which rock is a method of rebellion couldn't have chosen a less resonant time or theme. *Rock 'n' Roll High School* is aware of this, and therein lies its charm.

It's a musical comedy – a genre that all but died in the mid-1960s. However, a soundtrack featuring the Ramones, Devo and the Velvet Underground, among others, can't really be classified as a typical musical. It's a knowing homage to the Alan Freed movies of the 1950s (see, for example, *Go, Johnny, Go!* from 1958) and is strangely just as innocent as its 1950s predecessors. There is an endearing retro quality to this comedy: there are no drugs, the kids just want to rock and the Ramones ... well, they just want pizza.

The movie, aware of its own anachronistic themes, proceeds with tongue planted firmly in cheek and operates on a level of absurd fun. It exaggerates the villainy of its authority figures and reduces their disdain for rock to pathological obsession.

Riff Randell (P.J. Soles) is a surprisingly clean-cut Ramones fan. She's so exuberant, you don't care that she's obviously too old to still be in high school (this is complimented by casting the entire student body with mid-20s actors). Riff has penned a song for them and hopes to deliver it in person when they come to town.

Rounding up her pals Tom (Vincent Van Patten) and Eaglebauer (Clint Howard), Riff heads out to see the concert and meet her heroes in person. But the new iron-fisted principal at Vince Lombardi High, Miss Togar (Mary Woronov), has decided to declare all-out war on rock 'n' roll. Togar has even gone so far as to scientifically prove the damaging affects of rock by exposing lab mice to Ramones music. In a running gag, the mice become progressively more degenerate, donning little leather jackets and eventually exploding from the influence of the music. The teachers and parents hold a vinyl-fuelled bonfire and the outraged kids set out to teach the adults a lesson. With the help of the Ramones, they take over the school and rock 'n' roll mayhem ensues.

There are elements here that are cleverer than you might expect, including a few funny lines: 'Do your parents know you're Ramones?' 'Tom Roberts is so boring his brother is an only child'. Text-crawling the words to 'Teenage Lobotomy' across the bottom of the screen, a pair of overweight quasi-fascistic hall monitors and a teenage blackmarketeer operating out of a bathroom stall are the odd Tex Avery cartoonish details I love. You may recognise evil principal Mary Woronov and Paul Bartel (playing a deranged music teacher) as the couple later featured in the classic *Eating Raoul* (1982). Also, punk trivia nerds should look carefully during the live Ramones set for Darby Crash of The Germs in the front of the crowd.

Rock 'n' Roll High School is one of the few comedies put out by prolific horror and exploitation B-Movie mogul Roger Corman (*Voyage to the Planet of Pre-historic Women* (1966), Night Call Nurses (1972), *Grand Theft Auto* (1977)). Corman hired a young director named Allan Arkush who thankfully convinced Corman to change the name from 'Disco High' and use the Ramones as the featured band . The rest, as they say, is cult movie history and an excellent antidote to *Grease* (1978).

Gabba Gabba Hey!

▶▶

THE ROCKY HORROR PICTURE SHOW

Date:	1975
Director:	Jim Sharman
Writer(s):	Richard O'Brien, Jim Sharman
Runtime(s):	100 minutes
Country:	UK
Language:	English

DON'T DREAM IT, BE IT!

You may notice this book is arranged alphabetically. This choice comes from the simple fact that it is impossible to impose a hierarchy on a category as subjective as 'cult'. This movie is the single exception; it is the ultimate, quintessential and undisputed definition of a cult film. All cult films have some common aspects, but this is the only cult film I can think of that has all of them: it is a sci-fi, horror, parody, musical, bisexual glamrock extravaganza known as *The Rocky Horror Picture Show*.

Like many cult films, it was initially a box-office disappointment. Over time, audiences have appropriated the film, creating and sustaining the midnight-movie convention. As is the case with so many cult films, live viewing enhances the experience, but in this case it is essential. It is truly participant cinema, to the point where the communal spirit of viewing it has eclipsed the source material. The idea of reviving *Rocky Horror* live on Broadway seems counter-intuitive as it steals the action from the audience who own this classic. The film facilitates more interaction between audience members than it does with its own characters.

On a rainy night, a wholesome all-American couple, Janet (Susan Sarandon) and Brad (Barry Bostwick), have the unfortunate mishap of a flat tire near a castle occupied by a weird group of sundry sexual miscreants. Alpha freak is one Mr. Tim Curry, whose Dr. Frank N. Furter is a cinema icon – a mad scientist, alien, cult leader and lovesick transvestite in garter belts and torn stockings. Writer/composer Richard O'Brien plays Riff Raff, the Igor to Curry's Master, and were it not for Curry's character, O'Brien's would have dominated any other film. Notable other members of the family include the gorgeous Magenta (Patricia Quinn), the energetic Columbia (Nell Campbell) and a very young Meat Loaf in a fabulous cameo/musical number.

From there on, Frank N. Furter reveals his new creature Rocky (Peter Hinwood), kills his old one Eddie (Meat Loaf) and has sex with both Brad and Janet by trickery. Rocky escapes, returns to seduce Janet, and Dr. Everett Scott (Jonathan Adams) drops in. They all eat on top of Eddie's coffin and Columbia gets very upset. Everyone gets turned into statues, then there is a weird floor show.

The story is tied together through songs sung by the characters and narrator 'No Neck' (Charles Gray),who is seemingly in an omnipotent state of being. The film is meant to be high camp, but the songs – 'Science Fiction/Double Feature', 'Sweet Transvestite', 'Time Warp', 'Touch A Touch A Touch Me', 'Dammit Janet', 'Hot Patootie' and 'I'm Going Home' – are honestly better than parody would necessitate.

Ultimately it is Tim Curry's movie from start to finish. His character carries the film and drives the narrative flow. As the film ebbs and flows, so does he. Dr. Frank N. Furter switches wildly from camp queen to vicious leader to crumbling diva.

Curry's performance remains a spunky, full-throttle embrace of absolute pleasure. The songs remain rollicking, engaging and even beautifully melancholic – especially Frank's final tune in the film, 'Don't Dream It, Be It', which is so sad and yet so brilliant a coda.

I can never see it live without thinking of church. The film is after all more ritual than narrative. There is a kind of universal orthodoxy to viewing it, with the film serving as a kind of liturgy. Any line delivered by Janet or Brad is always greeted with 'Slut!' or 'Asshole!' respectively. The individual audiences provide the variations on weekend nights at midnight, in time zones the world over. There is recitation, singing and lots of sexual ambiguity, how catholic is that?

The audience took the theme 'Don't Dream It, Be It' to heart. The difference between seeing the film in a cinema and seeing it at home on video is comparable to the difference between pathetically watching pornography in private and taking part in a celebratory, 'Let your freak flag fly' parade. A word of warning, however: don't get carried away with yelling 'Slut!' every time Susan Sarandon comes on screen. It once got me thrown out of *Dead Man Walking*.

▶▶

ROGER AND ME

Date:	1989
Director:	Michael Moore
Writer(s):	Michael Moore
Runtime(s):	91 minutes
Country:	US
Language:	English

THE STORY OF A REBEL AND HIS MIKE.

Before making the 2002 Academy Award winner for Best Documentary *Bowling for Columbine,* director Michael Moore had already established his own style and created a sub-genre of documentary. The first in his body of work was 1989's *Roger and Me,* a genuinely subversive documentary that succeeds and endures by being one of the funniest films you will ever see. It was a bold shot across the bow of corporate practices in an allegedly prosperous America.

Journalist Michael Moore documents his efforts to obtain an interview with General Motors chairman Roger Smith. Between several unsuccessful attempts at meeting Smith, Moore turns his attention to the plight of his hometown of Flint, Michigan, which has been devastated by GM plant closings during Smith's tenure.

As someone who came of age in a dying Midwestern industrial town very much like Flint, Michigan (in my case Akron, Ohio), I can tell you the themes of bafflement, betrayal and despair associated with a corporation abandoning a loyal community are very resonant. Our region and condition were nearly invisible to the media save a few depressing pieces on the national news.

The beauty of Moore's documentation of Flint is that it is delivered with neither condescension nor pity. He is simply a resident with a camera. It is easy to see why the townspeople confided in him and the powerful were not intimidated. It would have been difficult to imagine that a 260lb man in an 'I'm Out for Trout' baseball cap was going to create a masterpiece on the class struggle in America.

The film works brilliantly in contrasts. It shifts between cocktail parties and evictions. We go from Anita Bryant telling us that anything is possible if you work hard and have faith in God, to a woman who sells rabbits 'As Pets or Meat'. We see the futile efforts of local government to turn a collapsing industrial town into a tourist attraction, while the local U-Haul can't keep up with demand with everyone wanting to leave.

Moore manages, without giving the impression that he is trying, to make the viewer feel his contempt for the vacuous celebrities, business leaders and politicians who offer useless advice to the workers left unemployed by the plant closings. This is a very funny movie, but also an extremely bitter one. It inspires not merely laughter, but a sense of outrage and moral indignation quite rare in film without seeming to preach or to distort what he records. He may have fiddled with the timeline presentation, but the focus remains intact. Smith's efforts to avoid the crew meant his abdication of the power to represent himself in the film. A role that Moore and company happily fulfil.

This film is *not* supposed to be an 'objective documentary'. It's the facts of the situation as seen by a kid who grew up in Flint among GM workers. He feels betrayed, he feels depressed and he feels angry. That's why the film has been called 'manipulative'. It's *Moore's* opinion! And even if it *is* his opinion, that doesn't excuse the behaviour of those who appear on camera without apology. Part of the validation of the film is in the vitriol conservative critics lodge against it as 'biased'. When considering this criticism, ask yourself how many car industry commercials you've seen, and how much they sought 'balance'.

The influence of *Roger and Me* is evident in Michael Moore's second documentary feature *The Big One* (1997). In the later film, Moore encounters much more receptive and savvy corporate public relations functionaries. These PR representatives appear to have been trained specifically and uniformly in 'What to do if Michael Moore shows up'. The previously mentioned *Bowling for Columbine* casts a wider net than simply going after a specific corporation or corporate America generally, but rather is a rumination on the culture of violence in America. Moore's work for TV is also worth exploring – *TV Nation* was a series of smaller investigative pieces based in the US, UK and Canada in the vein of *Roger and Me*, and is available as a video boxset.

Like any cult film, repeated viewings are advised. As much as the resonant themes, part of the appeal of the film are the odd incidental details inherent in a documentary. A careful read on the closing credits will reveal that Moore and company sustained filming by running a weekly bingo, whose participants they thank. The credits also inform us that 'the Flint plasma clinic is only open on Monday, Tuesday, Wednesday, Thursday, Friday and Saturday'. See the movie to laugh so that you may not weep.

▶▶

► # SKIDOO

Date:	1968
Director:	Otto Preminger
Writer(s):	Doran William Cannon
Runtime(s):	97 minutes
Country:	US
Language:	English

ALL YOU CAN DO IS SKIDOO...

Imagine the following cast in a single film: Jackie Gleason, Carol Channing, Frankie Avalon, Frank Gorshin, John Phillip Law, Peter Lawford, Burgess Meredith, George Raft, Cesar Romero, Austin Pendleton, Mickey Rooney and Groucho Marx. Seriously, take a moment and run down the list. Take your time, I'll wait ...

With that kind of talent combined with legendary director Otto Preminger (*Laura* (1944), *Exodus* (1960), *Man with the Golden Arm* (1955)), the logical conclusion is that for such a film to not be widely known it *had* to have been a disaster. It was. It is also reasonable to assume that when colossal talent fails, it fails colossally. It did. Welcome to the appeal of *Skidoo*, one of the strangest studio films ever made.

What can you say about a film whose final credits are sung? (I mean every credit, right down to 'gaffer'). A film where Groucho Marks plays a reclusive Mafia head named 'God'? And not least, a film where Jackie Gleason, 'The Great One', has an extended acid trip in prison? Well if you are the kind of person who would buy this book (and all evidence suggests that you are), then you would say 'I must see this film!'

Tony Banks (Jackie Gleason) is a retired mobster whittling away his days in comfortable boredom with his sexually restless wife Flo (Carol Channing). Their monotony is interrupted when a crime-kingpin called 'God' (Groucho Marx) recruits Tony to kill stool pigeon 'Blue Chips' Packard (Mickey Rooney). Packard is serving a life sentence, and the fact that Packard and Tony are lifelong friends complicates the assignment further.

It is after all 1968, and no comedy of the era would be complete without 'generation-gap-a-go-go'. The hippy counterculture is exemplified with as much depth as a 'Laugh-In' sketch by Banks' daughter Darlene (Alexandra Hay) and her friends, right down to body paint. Darlene's boyfriend (John Phillip Law in a role that proves his emotionally blank Angel in *Barbarella* was *not* artistic choice), explains that 'they're NOT digging the nine-to-five bag.'

Through a series of incidents, Tony manages to get himself locked up in a fully automated prison. His intellectual peacenik cellmate (Austin Pendleton) accidentally introduces Tony to LSD. This leads to a legendary sequence in which Jackie Gleason is sent on an acid trip of bizarre animation and terrified reaction shots. It culminates in Groucho Marx's head appearing on an animated screw to haunt 'The Great One'.

It gets better. You may have asked yourself why no one ever shot a scene in which Carol Channing seduces an aging teen heartthrob. Well, they did. Combining farce, disturbing menopausal aggression and a futuristic bachelor pad, Flo attempts to entice Marx's henchman Angie (Frankie Avalon). More unsettling still is that Angie seems genuinely aroused by her seizure of love. Fortunately they are interrupted in order to track down 'God' on the Howard Hughes-esque hermetically sealed yacht out in international waters, where he lives in limbo.

Meanwhile Tony and his cellmate escape by slipping LSD into the prison cafeteria food, consumed by all inmates, guards, the warden and a visiting Senator (Burgess Meredith and Peter Lawford). A particular pair of guards (Fred Clark and singer-songwriter Harry Nilsson, who also composed the soundtrack) hallucinate a musical number involving perfectly choreographed garbage cans while the two prisoners escape by homemade balloon.

They all converge on Groucho's ship for a final musical number, in which Carol Channing sings the *Skiddoo* theme song dressed in a naval motif.

I swear, I haven't made this up. When the establishment tries to make a counterculture film, it seldom succeeds. One of the great ironies of the studio system is that it is often blamed for squelching the freedom of daring newcomers. And yet the same system occasionally enables an artist of the stature of Preminger the carte blanche to make something this odd on this scale.

I am not a fan of the whole Schadenfreude/'so bad it's good' school of film appreciation. But this one is truly in a league of its own. Hearing that this movie exists is one thing, but the true surreality of its existence can only really be appreciated once you've actually *seen* it. It seems that everyone involved with the film sobered up and decided to quietly bury the evidence. Even today, few bad movie fans know of *Skidoo*. Reportedly, Preminger's daughter controls the negative and is sitting on it to protect her father's reputation. The forced obscurity has only whetted the cult interest. A late-70s issue of

High Times claims Groucho 'dropped' as a way of preparing for his role and had a pleasant experience. Nilsson said later in an interview that Marx had never used LSD at the time of filming but was merely drunk, an acting technique evident in nearly all aspects of this film.

▶▶

SLAP SHOT

Date:	1977
Director:	George Roy Hill
Writer(s):	Nancy Dowd
Runtime(s):	122 minutes
Country:	US
Language:	English

SLAP SHOT OUT SLAPS ... OUT SWEARS ... OUT LAUGHS ...

There have been quite a few sports films in cinema. And just like any other genre of film, sports films will inevitably produce subgenres and even cult films. Less popular than football, baseball and basketball in the US, and football in Europe, one could argue that hockey is kind of a 'cult sport'. Indeed the only country where hockey is the most popular sport, Canada, is itself a kind of 'cult country', a quirky little hybrid of the US and UK. What hockey lacks in numbers is made up for by the voraciousness of its fans.

The clincher for including *Slap Shot* in this book occurred in 2000 when I saw cultish sports fanaticism and cult film appreciation intersect. A full 23 years after the film's release, three fans at an Edmonton Oilers hockey game came dressed as 'the Hanson brothers', iconic characters from *Slap Shot*.

Paul Newman plays Reggie Dunlop, the player-coach of a minor-league hockey team called the Charlestown Chiefs. His team is in danger of folding because the owner is cheap, attendance is low and the local mill in the city is closing down. This film brings back memories of the mid-70s recession on

'The Rustbelt' of the American Northeast; depression and despondence brought on by the economy and the fact that your mediocre sports team does nothing to distract you.

There are plenty of colourful other characters here. Denis the goalie (Yvon Barrette) is a French-Canadian who speaks in hilarious broken English and claims to be 'allergic to the fans'. Ned Braden (Michael Ontkean), a Princeton graduate who's on the team so he can still play hockey despite the objections of his wife (Lindsay Crouse). And of course, the aforementioned Hanson brothers (Jeff Carlson, Steve Carlson and David Hanson), three goons who introduce a brand of hockey that turns around the fortunes of The Chiefs.

Slap Shot takes the time to investigate an array of pro-sports themes: sadistic player violence; boorish sexuality; fan behaviour; fan loyalty to athletes and vice-versa (or total absence thereof); and the bloodless, detached world of athletic club ownership. But the film is better than the snide satire it has been portrayed to be and, in its own manic way, it conveys much of the joy of sports. Certain storylines were still possible in the 1970s. Flawed heroes, societal critique and non-formulaic plots where characters might not necessarily win or might experience an ambiguous 'losing while winning' inconclusive ending. Sports, as an extension of those values, was as ripe as any other institution for a teardown.

On the surface, it is a comedy about a small losing hockey team and how they turn their luck by the use of violence. With this new tactic, they end up attracting fans and critics and disorienting rivals as the team rises to the top. The characterisations are vivid. Paul Newman's role is one of his best performances; multifaceted and complex. He is a manipulative, romantic, womanising, workaholic leader and father figure.

His two motivations, to win back his wife, who is about to divorce him, and to keep the team afloat, are almost in direct opposition to each other. To make matters worse, his character's instincts are often at odds with both goals.

The scenes are terribly realistic, the dialogue is memorable and, except for the fights in the ice, the comedy is never less than sublime. There's excellent slapstick humour to be sure, but there are also some great lines that fans of the movie will probably repeat forever. Michael Ontkean on the ice at the end is simply not to be missed.

This may also be one of the best 'guy films' ever made; it is crude, vulgar, scatological and authentic – and all written by a woman! To recognise her gender is not meant to take anything away from Nancy Dowd as a gifted comedic writer. But it is worth noting that the film is much more textured than might be expected. The relationships portrayed are not perfunctory love interests, and are not resolved in any manner resembling typical Hollywood treatment. They are complicated, frustrating and ring true. Particularly compelling is the relationship between Newman and his estranged wife (Jennifer Warren). They have affection and heartache and despite that recognise there are simply things two people can never resolve. Also, the isolation of the wives of the other players, who endure cheating and struggle with drinking and divorce is expressed poignantly. It's a real reflection of the dark side of our society at large; an analogy of the struggle between work and family, between professional and personal success.

It's based on the North American Hockey League's Johnstown Jets (still in existence as the Johnstown Chiefs in the East Coast Hockey League). The team was at one point coached by Steve Carlson (Steve Hanson in the movie) who, along with his brother Jack Carlson (who was originally meant to be playing Jack Hanson), went on to play briefly in the NHL. There was no third brother. Note: Jack Carlson had 248 penalty minutes in 50 games with Johnstown in 1974–75.

Paul Newman has repeatedly called *Slap Shot* one of his best efforts and, in interviews over the years, he has maintained that it was one of his favourite films to work on. Anyone who sees the joy of the entire cast in this wonderful little effort will find that easy to believe.

▶▶

SULLIVAN'S TRAVELS

Date:	1941
Director:	Preston Sturges
Writer(s):	Preston Sturges
Runtime(s):	90 minutes
Country:	US
Language:	English

VERONICA LAKE'S ON THE TAKE.

In this book I have referred to films that are cults within a specific group (for example *Network* is a cult film among journalists). *Sullivan's Travels* repeatedly shows up on the cult lists of people who honestly love movies. Were it more widely popular, *Sullivan's Travels* would be considered a classic. It's post-modern before its time. It's self-referential, as one of the first movies about making movies. Its command of irony and pathos is so sophisticated you will have trouble believing it was made in 1941.

John L. Sullivan (Joel McCrea), a feature film director known for screwball comedies, becomes disenchanted with his work and decides he wants to make serious films in the vein of John Steinbeck. He talks about the transcendent nature of film as an art that can educate and speak to people on an emotional level. His studio humours his dilettantism, confident that he will become frustrated in his search and return defeated to make more comedies. He's soon joined by a very lovely and devoted Veronica Lake, who thinks that he's someone down on his luck.

Sullivan genuinely attempts to give up his pampered life, preferring to wander and live by his wits. However his producers refuse to leave him alone, sending a high-tech fleet after him, equipped with doctors, cooks, writers and PR people. Also, no matter how hard he tries, Sullivan ends up back in Hollywood every time.

Sullivan returns to the road to repay the acts of kindness shown to him by fellow travellers when he is attacked, suffers amnesia and ends up working on a chain gang after being convicted of assault. There he learns the real meaning of hardship and has second thoughts about making his realistic magnum opus. In the penultimate realisation that 'the journey *is* the destination', Sullivan experiences poverty first hand, and recognises his relationship to society and obligation as an artist.

One cannot do justice to the brilliance with which the characters, situations and themes of this film intersect without giving away the joy of surprise. *Sullivan's Travels* is a very unpredictable film, and therein lies a great deal of its charm. We do not expect a film nearly as funny, sweet or profound as it ends up being.

The first third is a brilliant screwball comedy, the second third is a romantic buddy picture and the final third is a moving drama. On his journey he learns much about himself and society, falls in love and arrives at an epiphany. The journey affirms everything he espoused, with an opposite conclusion. The dramatic portions are sometimes moving, sometimes unsettling. It offers a dizzying pastiche of styles and genres, including dialogue worthy of Noel Coward, slapstick on a par with the Marx brothers and muckraker grit and outrage worthy of H.L. Mencken. It's a difficult balance to maintain and in lesser hands it would have deteriorated.

One of Sturges's greatest attributes was his ability to write women. I cannot overstate how rare that was in his era, particularly in comedy. Women were usually foils for male characters, or else served as some kind of goal that the male characters struggle to attain. In Sturges's films women are fully realised, complex and hilarious. Many attribute this to his mother, an elegant, funny, larger-than-life socialite. In *Sullivan's Travels* Veronica Lake (simply referred to as 'the Girl') is stunning. I am not just referring to her remarkable beauty. I mean the performance is a comedic *tour de force*.

There is a bit of a cult following to all Preston Sturges's impressive body of work; *The Lady Eve* (1941), *The Great McGinty* (1940), *The Palm Beach Story* (1942), *Hail the Conquering Hero* (1944), *The Miracle of Morgan's Creek* (1944) and *Unfaithfully Yours* (1948). All are great films and all contain elements of his genius. He has a signature directing style and faithfully employs a regular ensemble of character actors: Robert Warwick (Mr. Lebrand), William Demarest (Mr. Jones), Franklin Pangborn (Mr. Casalsis), Porter Hall (Mr. Hadrian), Byron Foulger (Mr. Valdelle), Margaret Hayes (Secretary), Robert Greig (Sullivan's Butler) and Eric Blore (Sullivan's Valet). But it is *Sullivan's Travels* with its revolutionary and effective self-reflective take on Hollywood and the nature of comedy that makes it stand out. It is difficult enough to produce effective comedy and social commentary. To weave the two so well is brilliance.

▶▶

SUSPIRIA

Date:	1977
Director:	Dario Argento
Writer(s):	Dario Argento, Daria Nicolodi and Thomas De Quincey (book *Suspiria de Profundis*, uncredited)
Runtime(s):	98 minutes
Country:	Italy, West Germany
Language:	English, German, Latin

THE ONLY THING MORE TERRIFYING THAN THE LAST 12 MINUTES OF THIS FILM ARE THE FIRST 92.

Popular wisdom states that we can only dream in black and white. Anyone who swears that they dream in colour will appreciate Dario Argento's *Suspiria*. It may be the closest anyone has yet come to filming a nightmare, a nightmare of stunning colour and rich imagery.

Opinions on *Suspiria* are almost always passionate, ranging from masterpiece to dreck. It is considered by many to be the greatest Italian horror film, at least comparable to Mario Bava's masterpiece *La Maschera del Demonio* (1960). What is indisputable is that the film has garnered a cult following that has only grown over 25 years.

Suspiria is nearly perfect in form. That's not to say that the content is perfect. It isn't, not by a long shot. But there is nothing about this film that doesn't belong. Everything fits – music, action, editing. Every facet comes together fantastically, resulting in a hellish fairy tale brimming with hallucinatory panic and suffocating tension. The rhythm stands out particularly. Argento establishes moments of high tension and then lets you relax long enough to be jarred again.

The tagline for *Suspiria*, 'The only thing more terrifying than the last 12 minutes of this film are the first 92' is an interesting claim. The first twelve minutes are so breathtaking, thrilling, enthralling and scary that you'll wonder how he can top them. He doesn't. But by imbuing the opening sequence with as much action as the climax of most films, he creates tension and expectation, elements more vital to truly effective horror than gore or action. The fear is not merely of a specified entity, but of some nameless dread, a sense of all-pervading evil.

The plot, such as it is, involves American ballet dancer Suzy (Jessica Harper) arriving in Germany to attend a prestigious ballet academy during torrential rain. As her taxi drives her nearer the remote school, she witnesses a girl running in horror through a forest in the opposite direction. Suzy meets Madam Blanc (Joan Bennett) the headmistress, and one of the teachers, Miss Tanner (Alida Valli). Upon making friends with a girl named Sara (Stefania Casini), Suzy learns that all is not quite as it seems and that the academy is a mere front for a coven of witches headed by mysterious Master Suspiriorum.

Argento and cinematographer Luciano Tovoli create powerful and highly original effects with complex camera movements and wild angles. But *Suspiria*'s photography is mainly about colours. It is one of the last features to use Technicolor and one of the earliest innovators in the use of gels. Thus, the startlingly designed sets were bathed in very deep reds and blues, creating a hallucinatory atmosphere, a kind of perverse *Hansel and Gretel*.

Claudio Simonetti and his band Goblin produce a soundtrack consisting of whispers and exotic instruments. They have composed atmospheric music for films like Argento's *Profondo Rosso* (1975), George Romero's *Dawn of the Dead* (1978) and Luigi Cozzi's *Contaminazione* (1980). In *Suspiria* they create a theme that runs from the opening credits to the final frame.

Written by Argento and his future wife Daria Nicolodi, the premise for *Suspiria* allegedly comes from an incident involving Nicolodi's grandmother, a famous pianist. She claims to have auditioned at a music academy that was a front for black magic. Nicolodi refuses to tell the name of the academy claiming 'reasons of safety'. Whether true or hoax, it adds a brilliant mystique to the film.

▶▶

Taxi Driver

Date:	1976
Director:	Martin Scorsese
Writer(s):	Paul Schrader
Runtime(s):	113 minutes, 110 minutes (Spain)
Country:	USA
Language:	English

ON EVERY STREET IN EVERY CITY, THERE'S A
NOBODY WHO DREAMS OF BEING A SOMEBODY.

Taxi Driver had a definite impact on filmmaking, but also on culture at large. Ronald Reagan's 1981 would-be assassin, John Hinckley, cited his obsession with actress Jodi Foster's role in this film as his prime motivation for shooting the President. *Taxi Driver* was nominated for 4 Oscars and won 0, including a loss to *Rocky* for best picture.

De Niro delivers one of cinema's iconic performances:

> **'You talking to me? Are you talking to me?**
> **I don't see anyone else here.'**

It is that last line that is key. There *is* no one else to take action. There is no indignation more righteous than that of the reluctant hero. The role is morally ambiguous but somehow still intense.

Travis Bickle is a Vietnam veteran who cannot sleep. He decides to drive a taxicab on the nightshift. As Travis drives around New York City, his disgust and anger ferments. When this film came out, New York was not having a good period and it looked like hell. Literally like hell, thanks to the stunning cinematography of Michael Chapman, with steam rising in a haze of blurred red lights.

A cab driver is the ultimate voyeur; present, serving a function, seemingly non-judgmentally. People do not generally feel compelled to monitor their behaviour in front of drivers, and Bickle sees all. He moves through this landscape nearly invisible, seems to have distance between himself and others at every turn. He is surrounded by pornography, but seems sexually ambivalent. Sex is perhaps degraded to Bickle by the perverse manifestations of the element with whom he comes into contact.

Over time Bickle recognises himself as more than a simple observer, he is a participant in the foulness, an enabler who moves these elements to and from their transgressions. He recognises in himself something akin to 'sins of omission' whereby one who witnesses vice but doesn't speak out or act against it is complicit. Making Bickle a Vietnam vet gives him a pretext of disenchantment and a proficiency in lethal force. The character has begun with a certain trajectory, and a sense of urgency and mission builds.

He also seems to have a desperate need to make some kind of human contact – to somehow share or mimic the effortless social interaction he sees all around him. He is drawn to the respectable world, wishing in part to offset his familiarity with the underside. Travis becomes infatuated with a beautiful campaign worker named Betsy (Cybill Shepherd), and he persuades her to go on a date with him. Betsy is clearly intrigued by Travis, or perhaps by what he represents, so she agrees. Travis makes the mistake of taking her to an X-rated movie. His socialisation is completely out of sorts.

Bickle develops disdain for the politician for whom Betsy works. This animosity seems to arise not only from the politician riding in Bickle's cab with a prostitute, but from Bickle's sense of accountability. To Bickle, one who presides ineffectually over a cesspool is indictable. Travis slowly plans and prepares himself, but for what action he is not clear. It is rather the compulsion to act, a manifestation of rage that has yet to take form. In a classic exchange of dialogue with a fellow cab driver named Wizard (Peter Boyle), Travis shows signs of psychosis. Bickle's journal of progress, expressed in voiceover narration, chronicles the revelation: 'Here is a man who cannot take it anymore' and 'Loneliness has followed me all my life'.

Travis comes very near assassinating the politician, but his motives and outlets shift abruptly. Instead he focuses on a 12-year-old prostitute named Iris (Jody Foster). Bickle develops a paternal protectiveness toward Iris and focuses on saving her, even if she hasn't expressed a specific desire to have him do so. As Travis tries to convince Iris to give up prostitution, she manages to keep a steady face but clearly is suffering inside. Travis' emotion is clearly anger but he tries to hold it because he does not want to scare Iris. Foster and De Niro play the scene with wonderful realism and emotion. Bickle focuses his rage on her pimp, Sport (Harvey Keitel). It is a direct homage to the classic John Ford Western *The Searchers* (1956), in which a character named Ethan, played by John Wayne, is in a desperate search for his niece abducted by an Indian named Scar. Scorsese traces the events that lead to the release of Iris. The main characters in both films are lonely wanderers and war veterans.

The film's conclusion intentionally lacks finality. We hear a letter from Iris's parents, the Steensmas, being read across images of Bickle convalescing, yet we sense no justice. The letter from the Steensmas thanks him for saving their girl. But a crucial earlier scene between Iris and Sport suggests that she was content to be with him, and the reasons why she ran away from home are not explored.

Is Travis a psychopath? That depends on how you judge someone who chooses to not fit in with a corroded social fabric. I think Scorsese's intention is to continually draw a fine line between his motives and behaviour. The movie is mostly about hypocrisy. He doesn't lie, he's not afraid, he's protective towards the exploited and emerges as one of the few people in the city prepared to act on his morals. Running alongside this is the fact that society views his sanity as borderline because of his unwillingness to remain a voyeur.

Violence may be an instrument for dispensing 'justice' – ie, by ending a life – but it has no power to resolve life's complexities or relieve its pain.

Scorsese surrounds De Niro with a first-rate supporting cast, including Harvey Keitel, Peter Boyle, Albert Brooks, Jodie Foster and Cybill Shepherd, and the underrated Victor Argo and Joe Spinell. Scorsese himself has a nice cameo as a passenger teetering on the verge of homicide who confides in Bickle.

Bernard Herrmann, who died shortly after completing the score, provides a melancholy feeling to the movie. The haunting jazz sax seems to be sounding an elegy for the numerous wandering shells, seen through the eyes of Robert De Niro's own disturbed character.

▶▶

THE TEXAS CHAIN SAW MASSACRE

Date:	1974
Director:	Tobe Hooper
Writer(s):	Kim Henkel and Tobe Hooper
Runtime(s):	83 minutes, 75 minutes (Germany, new longer version)
Country:	USA
Language:	English

WHO WILL SURVIVE AND WHAT WILL BE LEFT OF THEM?

Wisconsin serial killer Ed Gein was a necrophiliac and devotee of the wartime Nazi concentration camp medical experiments. On one occasion, he plundered a Wisconsin graveyard by night for edible body parts, and flayed one corpse to fashion a waistcoat souvenir. Some time later, when police called at his house to question Gein about a missing elderly woman, they discovered the gutted torso of one of his earlier female victims hanging from the beams.

In a case as bizarre and brutal as the Gein case, it is difficult for art to surpass life. His macabre deeds in the late 1950s are thought to have inspired the Alfred Hitchcock thriller *Psycho* (1960) and two low-budget horror movies *Deranged* (1974) and *Three on a Meat Hook* (1972).

The Texas Chain Saw Massacre was the first film to declare the Ed Gein case as an overt influence. But I must warn you not to let the title fool you into thinking there is a positive social message in transplanting the story from Wisconsin to Texas; the film involves a massacre *by* Texans not *of* Texans.

This is the one that started it all, from the masked murderer concept to a cannibalistic family. Director Tobe Hooper created the pinnacle of American horror, bringing real fear and a slight hint of dark humour, while commenting on the breakdown of the American family. It's a sort of brutal synthesis of the Manson Family and the Ed Gein case.

The movie starts with a group of friends, Sally Hardesty (Marilyn Burns), her disabled brother Franklin (Paul A. Partain), Jerry, Kirk and Pam travelling through rural Texas. They are en-route to a graveyard to see if the graves of Sally and Franklin's grandparents were defiled in a rash of robberies.

They meet a weird hitchhiker (Edwin Neal) who proceeds to freak out when Franklin ruminates on how they kill cows at slaughterhouses. The hitchhiker is thrown out of the van.

Eventually the journey ends in an abandoned family home. To make a long story short, and in accordance with American horror convention, one by one (and in some cases by two) the characters wander off, end up at an old house and meet up with the infamous Leatherface (Gunnar Hansen) and his family. All the males are wasted quickly (both early on, and in lightning fast assaults), while the women are tortured slowly and methodically. And so you only hope that our last remaining girl survives or dies quickly so that her misery is over.

The movie was made on a shoestring budget and the product reflects that. However, I believe in this instance it adds to the 'brute force' of the film. The grainy feel adds a priceless raw atmosphere.

The disturbing tones in the film can be very subtle. Look and listen for them. The detail in the cannibals' home is amazing. And pay close attention to the slaughterhouse and barbecue references that are subtly placed throughout the film. And you have to love that glowing lampshade at the dinner table. Unfortunately, this is made difficult as the DVD version is somewhat darkly lit and does not do justice to the original. The VHS versions are slightly better but really, to appreciate this film, you need to get hold of a 16 or 35mm film print, and see just how Hooper meant the scenes inside the house to be seen.

Marilyn Burns gives a thrilling performance as Sally. She screams and screams and screams. But it isn't typical 'crap b-movie screaming'; it feels total, committed and real, particularly at the end in the gas station where she delivers her shock very believably. But a bit of instructional advice from the film: if you're being chased by a crazed, chainsaw-wielding maniac through a dark wood, the last thing you want to do is scream and give away your position.

The fact that barely a pint of blood is spilt onscreen is astonishing. There's a very little visible violence in this film, but the atmosphere of sheer dread and terror is simply overwhelming. It's a study in the art of suggestion, a movie that is so outrageous and demented you never notice how subtly it reels you in.

▸▸

THIS IS SPINAL TAP

Date:	1984
Director:	Rob Reiner
Writer(s):	Christopher Guest, Michael McKean, Harry Shearer and Rob Reiner
Runtime(s):	82 minutes
Country:	USA
Language:	English

DOES FOR ROCK AND ROLL WHAT THE SOUND OF MUSIC DID FOR HILLS.

I hate parody. What I should have said is I hate bad parody. Because 99 per cent of the time they are smug, obvious and artistically lazy exercises that merely mirror the structure of an existing subject to make referential jokes. Parody can work, but for that to happen you must not simply know your subject, you must love it.

The brilliant Eric Idle film *The Rutles* (1977) was structurally similar to legitimate Beatles documentaries and clearly based on love for its subject matter. Nigel Innes so gorgeously mimicked The Beatles that *The Rutles*' soundtrack stands up to any real Mersey Beat act.

This Is Spinal Tap works gloriously for the same reason, and I would say that it goes even further. The film is so richly inhabited it is a phenomenon itself. It has 'killer' tracks like 'Stonehenge', 'Big Bottom' and 'Rock 'n' Roll Creation', and the lyrics themselves are enough to have you falling out of your seat.

The real authenticity of *Spinal Tap* lies not in the film so closely resembling a documentary, rather it comes from portraying the members of Spinal Tap as bad musicians, not bad men. Some artists have even gone so far to say that they learned how to be a rock star from *Spinal Tap* as much as from their own success.

Filmmaker Marty DiBergi (Rob Reiner), taking a break from dog food commercials, is determined to capture the sights, sounds and smells of his favourite rock group, the legendary Spinal Tap, on their latest US tour. They're a 20-year-old heavy metal outfit from England centring around lead singer David St. Hubbins (Michael McKean), lead guitarist Nigel Tufnel (Christopher Guest) and bass guitarist Derek Smalls (Harry Shearer). The rest of the band is a revolving door of personnel including a series of unlucky drummers (including Mick Shrimpton, who is played by R. J. Parnell) who have met with bizarre ends:

Marty DiBergi:	**So what happened to that drummer?**
Mick Shrimpton:	**Well, it's also not a very pleasant story but ... well, he died.**
Derek Smalls:	**Yeah. The official explanation is that he choked ... on vomit.**
Mick:	**In fact, it was someone else's vomit, but they don't know exactly whose vomit it was. They, they don't have the technology at Scotland Yard to ... you know, find out for sure or anything.**
Nigel Tufnel:	**You can't ... dust for vomit.**

The tour is the first the band has made of America in years. When asked if smaller venues represent diminishing popularity, manager Ian Faith (Tony Hendra) quickly dismisses the idea. The band's fans are just becoming more 'selective', he says. Still, the group is received well at their initial shows – those that haven't been cancelled. The tour is one disaster after another. Stage props malfunction, the band can't find its way to the stage from their dressing rooms ('Hello Cleveland!') and fans don't show up for autograph sessions at record stores. Radio stations play their oldies and ask, 'Where are they now?' David's girlfriend Jeanine (June Chadwick), the band's Yoko Ono, arrives – much to the consternation of Nigel, who has a crush on David, which is obvious to everyone *but* David. Jeanine begins making unsolicited contributions, such as having the band dress in fantasy creature costumes and recording their music 'in Dubly'.

The band feel things will pick up if they can just get their new album released. But Polymer Records refuses to distribute *Smell the Glove* because of its sexist cover art ('What's wrong wit be'n "sexy"?'). Eventually it's released with a solid black record sleeve, a reverse of The Beatles' White Album in appearance, artistic merit and sales. The band sinks so low as to be billed second to a puppet show at a theme park. The pressures mount as the tour limps to a close.

Throughout, we're treated to the band's rock and roll wisdom and philosophy. Nigel informs Marty of one of the reasons for their success – loud amplifiers. While the volume settings on other bands' equipment might just go to 10, theirs goes to 11! Asked if there's really a difference, Nigel replies, 'Yeah, well it's like ... one louder, innit?'

Aside from appearing in the film, Guest, McKean, Shearer

CULT MOVIES IN SIXTY SECONDS

and Reiner wrote the screenplay themselves, benefiting from improvisational rehearsals. They also wrote all the songs, some of which, like 'Sex Farm', became popular and were really not much worse than other heavy metal hits. It's a fantastic testament to this film that a parody of a Glam band on the skids retains more popularity now than all the bands that were popular when the film was made. People remember the parody but not the subject matter.

The film defined much of the 'mockumentary' genre that followed. The later directorial work of Christopher Guest has included the mockumentaries *Waiting for Guffman* (1996) and *Best in Show* (2000).

The performances are solid with surprisingly good accent work from Americans. The supporting roles are gold as well. Tony Hendra plays cricket bat toting manager Ian Faith, who wearily absorbs the band's abuse even as he protects them. Angelica Houston plays Polly Deutsh, a set designer with a problem distinguishing dimensions. Fred Willard is the master of taking a small role and making it more memorable than it deserves. Here he plays upbeat Airforce officer Lt. Hookstratten, who disastrously books the band to play an officers' dance.

The fact that the members of Spinal Tap actually appeared live with orchestral accompaniment to perform 'Bitch School' at the opening for the 1998 Annual Meeting of the National Organization of Women will forever refute that feminism is humourless.

Spinal Tap viewers agree that this one goes to '11'.

▶▶

180

TRAINSPOTTING

Date:	1996
Director:	Danny Boyle
Writer(s):	Irvine Welsh (novel), John Hodge
Runtime(s):	94 minutes
Country:	UK
Language:	English

CHOOSE LIFE. CHOOSE A JOB. CHOOSE A STARTER HOME. CHOOSE DENTAL INSURANCE, LEISURE WEAR AND MATCHING LUGGAGE. CHOOSE YOUR FUTURE. BUT WHY WOULD ANYONE WANT TO DO A THING LIKE THAT?

Trainspotting started out as a cult Scottish novel, was adapted to a West End play, and became a wildly successful ensemble film of lovely character driven performances. Jonny Lee Miller is the absolute perfect Sick Boy and Ewan McGregor is brilliant as Renton, Ewen Bremner is hilarious as Spud and Robert Carlyle is an amazing Begbie. Even novelist Irvine Welsh makes a cameo appearance as drug dealer, Mother Superior, who according to Renton is 'called that on account of the length of his habit'.

Acts of insanity and perverse clarity compete for dominance in a film that is by turns visceral, sublime, subtle and outrageous. Its stylistic exuberance, its visual inventiveness and its sheer energy heighten throughout. Characters fight for 'life' where life or living is anathema. It mixes despondency with humour, bleakness with wit, and bitter realism with surrealistic fantasy.

Poignant, hilarious, harrowing and upbeat in turns, it presents believable, rounded characters instead of the one-sided caricatures so often portrayed in drug films.

The film opens with a voice-over narration from Renton while he and geeky, gawky Spud, dash down the street pursued by security guards who've caught them shoplifting. It's an underbelly variation on the opening of *A Hard Day's Night*. Renton's speech begins to move to the dual rhythms of his hurtle along the pavement and Iggy Pop's 'Lust for Life'. A minute later, we're in a flat watching Sick Boy, whose bleached blond hair and suavity make him just a bit better-looking and therefore 'functional' than a heavy user should appear, prepare a shot for Allison (Susan Vidler).

We see the life of the user: the terrible, the shocking and the banal. Sometimes all concurrently. Boyle really lets loose in a couple of expressionist sequences, including one where Renton dives headfirst into 'the filthiest toilet in Scotland' to retrieve two opium suppositories and emerges beneath the ocean's surface where the evacuated drugs gleam like gems on the sea floor. The scene is almost unbearable; but what an example of what it means to be in thrall to drugs. In the most notorious scene, we see the corpse of Allison's baby daughter, dead from neglect, a casualty of everyone else's self-involvement. And there's a mind-boggling section where Renton's parents lock him in his bedroom to go cold turkey and he imagines the trains on his childhood wallpaper chugging past him, his parents on a game show answering questions about HIV infection, and the dead baby girl crawling along the ceiling, pausing to stare at him accusingly. The sequence makes you feel like you're suffering along, even as you're marvelling at its technique.

The reputation of the film was widespread. During the 1996 American Presidential campaign, Republican candidate Bob Dole criticised *Trainspotting* for glorifying heroin abuse. In a later clarification, he admitted he hadn't seen it.

The movie's unsentimental, non-judgmental view of heroin addiction is summed up by lead character Mark Renton in the film's opening sequence: 'I chose not to choose life. I chose somethin' else. And the reasons? There are no reasons. Who needs reasons when you've got heroin?' The escalation of this plays out in a practical joke that Renton plays on his pal Tommy (Kevin McKidd) a poor, simple, trusting, non-user. It winds up costing Tommy his girlfriend. Desolate, Tommy offers to pay Renton to shoot him up, and Renton, needing money to score, agrees – getting Tommy hooked.

Trainspotting never descends into moralism or judgement. Like Gus Van Sant's *Drugstore Cowboy* (1989), it treats the addicts like human beings. These people laugh, cry, suffer and try to make sense of their lives. As Irvine Welsh himself said, 'If you're not an addict there's a temptation to imagine them as being monsters or freaks or mutants. But we can all go there in different ways. The book brings it back into focus that these people are part of our society.' The audience must identify with Renton for the film to work. Without that connection, much of the message of this film would be lost.

According to Danny Boyle: 'In an old-fashioned message film, Renton would be destroyed in the end, because he's a terrible abuser, a despicable person in some ways. Instead he slides away. And yet the nicest guy in the whole film, and the last to use, is the first to die. There is no fairness, but there is plenty of mayhem.'

There's a script in circulation which is a good source for those who have difficulty deciphering the movie's thick Scottish brogue. The *Trainspotting* soundtrack is spectacular (Heaven 17, New Order, Iggy Pop, Blur, Beethoven, Leftfield, Pulp). It was a bestseller, putting Iggy Pop's 'Lust for Life' on the map. It's hilarious to hear a song about heroin addiction appropriated for so much mainstream corporate advertising. But why would anyone want to do a thing like that?

▶▶

VALLEY OF THE DOLLS

Date:	1967
Director:	Mark Robson
Writer(s):	Helen Deutsch, Dorothy Kingsley,
	Jacqueline Susann (novel)
Runtime(s):	123 minutes
Country:	US
Language:	English

THE NATION'S MOST STARTLING AND HOTLY
DISCUSSED BESTSELLER NOW ON THE
SCREEN WITH EVERY
SHOCK AND SENSATION INTACT.

**'I'm Neely O'Hara, pal! That's me singin' on
that jukebox!'**

Valley of the Dolls is a masterpiece of miscalculation. That is
not a backhanded insult; I mean the film is truly remarkable in
the consistency of its camp. Rarely has plot, dialogue, casting
and music all failed with such coordinated singularity of
purpose to coalesce into an icon. I would have sworn *Valley of
the Dolls* was workshopped by a drag queen theatre ensemble in
a marathon of 'bigger equals better' performance. However, the
Jacqueline Susann novel that preceded the film is one of the
bestselling novels of all time.

The plot, such as there is one, is the ultimate showbusiness
horror tale. *Valley* depicts what happens to three nice girls when
they become famous and start taking pills or 'dolls'.

Anne Welles (Barbara Parkins) leaves the snowfall of New

England for the slush of New York. She immediately ends up with the dream job for a pre-feminist era Vassar girl, as a secretary, and meets Mr. Heartthrob, Lyon (Paul Burke, who employs the interesting acting choice of talking about being British instead of actually using a British accent). Anne tangles with the nasty grande dame of the theatre, Helen Lawson (Susan Hayward), and then becomes a supermodel overnight. You know, like you do.

Then there's Jennifer North (Sharon Tate), an aspiring actress who has a nice body but can't act. We know this bit of exposition because she is repeatedly shown on one side of a telephone conversation agreeing with her mother about her lack of talent. She too falls in love, with Tony Scotti (Tony Polar), a lounge entertainer with what sounds like the singer's version of a speech impediment. Tony also harbours a deep, dark secret which somehow drives Jennifer to get naked in French cinema.

And then there is Neely O'Hara (Patty Duke) the kid 'who's really got it' (talent that is). Neely walks out 'with dignity' from Ms. Lawson's show after it is clear she's a threat to the aging star. She claws her way to the top, singing some of the worst songs written for the screen. Her fame evaporates into pills, booze and divorce. She somehow ends up in the same sanatorium as Jennifer's boyfriend, returns to defile Ms. Lawson's wig and delivers a near career-ender of a final scene. We also get Duke's delivery of 'Goodbye pussycat, me-yoow.' and a pool scene with: 'How dare you contaminate my pool. Here – maybe this'll disinfect it.'

Meanwhile the men in this film – Paul Burke, Charles Drake, Tony Scotti and Martin Milner – seem handpicked for their blandness. They are essentially the slices of white bread between which a self-destructive female sturm and drang sandwich is made. But that's how the source material is laid out, and excepting the male leads, the sledgehammer direction, overripe acting and eyepopping fashions are true to the Jackie Susann oeuvre.

Even as 'controversial' as the film was in its time, the film omits plotlines such as Jennifer's lesbian affair, Tony's preference for 'backdoor deliveries' and Neely walking in on Ted Casablanca with another man. It's speculated that Jacqueline Susann based the character of Neely O'Hara on Judy Garland. In fact, Judy Garland was signed to play Helen Lawson, but sadly the actress was too busy living her own trainwreck to participate in this one, and was replaced by Susan Hayward.

And if you feel the film alone lacks a 'laugh-that-I-may-not-weep' quality, check out *Patty Duke Sings Songs From Valley of The Dolls & Other Selections* (1968) where she sings her own off-key renditions of songs from the movie. It seems Patty did not do her own singing in the film. Listen and find out why.

It is a quintessential, 1960s time capsule. Everything from Anne's lipstick shade (barely pink) to the George Nelson chairs in her modern home. It is also an entertaining piece of cinematic trash that is nowhere near as racy as it would like us to believe; and that's part of its twisted charm. Because it fails on so many levels – as true art, as explicitly sexual titillation or as a faithful adaptation of a popular book – it's downright inspiring that it comes together so well. *Valley of the Dolls'* ultimate triumph is that, despite its incredible waste of talent, time and money, 30 years later we're still watching. Even those of us who aren't gay males.

▶▶

THE WARRIORS

Date:	1979
Director:	Walter Hill
Writer(s):	Sol Yurick (novel) David Shaber, and Walter Hill
Runtime(s):	93 minutes
Country:	US
Language:	English

THESE ARE THE ARMIES OF THE NIGHT!

There is much to say so, 'Let's get down to it Boppers ...'

Hundreds of NYC gangs from all five boroughs show up for a summit at the Bronx Zoo, where Cyrus (Roger Hill), the Bismarck/Garibaldi of the late-1970s gang world, is holding a meeting. He dreams of uniting all the gangs in a bid to take over the city (this is not contested by anyone, least of all the New York City Police Department), or, as he puts it, 'We have the streets suckas ... can you dig it?' This dream is shattered by an assassin's bullet. A gang called The Warriors are wrongly accused of murdering Cyrus. Essentially, what follows is a plotline worthy of an Xbox video game (and that's a compliment); the gang must travel all the way from the Bronx Zoo to their home turf of Coney Island without being eliminated by the rival gangs. Each gang has their own strengths, weaknesses and 'themes' – there are guys in greasepaint and baseball uniforms, zoot suits, skinheads and yes even mimes. The Warriors hold their own in several extremely well choreographed fight scenes, including one in a subway station bathroom that reportedly took a week to film.

It's a modern adaptation of *The Odyssey* wherein a Greek army had to make a difficult journey home from a foreign land. The baseball themed gang is called The Furies and a siren-esque all-female gang is known as The Lizzies. Lynne Thigpen appears intermittently as a radio DJ who imparts information to the gangs tracking The Warriors, and serves as a foxy, one-woman Greek chorus.

Swan (as played by Michael Beck later of *Xanadu* (1980) infamy), is The Warriors' hardened leader. He is cold, calculating, and only shows faint hints of emotion. Ajax (James Remar) the number two, has many of the same attributes, but is little more raw and brutal. While the villain, Luther (David Patrick Kelly), is just plain psychotic. When members of his own gang, The Rogues, question his motives, Luther responds simply, 'I just like doing stuff like that'. If you've ever wondered why someone would put beer bottles on each of their fingers and say, 'War-Ree-Ers, come out to play-ay', Luther is the reason. Once you see the film, that bit will finally make sense and be funny for once (but only once!)

Why cult? Because this movie is the premiere example of the urban fantasy adventure, with the emphasis on fantasy. The depiction of New York in the 1970s is not realistic so much as it is a vision of New York people had in the 1970s; the sum of all fears born of societal pessimism and too many cop shows. Deriding the film for its lack of 'realism' misses the point; you might as well pan *West Side Story* because real gangs don't dance.

This film has a cool, reluctant relationship to violence. These are not fights The Warriors want or even deserve. Likewise, you cannot vilify the rival gangs, as they think The Warriors are guilty of cold-blooded murder. This is not a movie about fighting but surviving. It's not about glorifying violence (vengeance, etc) it's about simply getting home. There is no gunplay in this film (save the assassination of Cyrus), rather the fights are all determined by strength and cunning.

It all ends with vindication at daybreak in Coney Island: 'You Warriors are good. Real good!' 'The best'. Finally, it goes out with our chorus/foxy DJ: 'The earlier reports were wrong, all wrong. Sorry about that. And for that group that had such a hard time getting home tonight, I guess all we can do is play you a song.'

Can you dig it? Oh yeah.

▶▶

THE WICKER MAN

Date:	1973
Director:	Robin Hardy (I)
Writer(s):	Anthony Shaffer
Runtime(s):	102 minutes
Country:	UK
Language:	English

FLESH TO TOUCH ... FLESH TO BURN! DON'T KEEP THE WICKER MAN WAITING!

The Wicker Man is a very atmospheric film but you can't pigeonhole it. Horror? Not quite. Murder mystery? Not exactly. It is more than any single genre. While defying simple definition makes for a studio marketing nightmare (which it was), it can make for the kind of distinctiveness to which cult audiences are drawn.

Edward Woodward plays Sergeant Howie, sent to the remote island of Summerisle off Scotland to investigate an anonymous report of a missing girl. He finds a strange and sometimes perverse sub-culture practising what appear to be ancient paganistic rituals. As a devout Christian, Howie is not only offended, but ruthlessly determined to get to the bottom of the mystery. Summerisle's inhabitants initially claim the child never existed, but Howie's implacable prying gradually leads him to believe she was murdered in a pagan sacrificial ritual.

The evidence of the islanders' ancient belief system are all around him: most of the film consists of him doggedly following a string of clues while bristling with righteous disgust over fertility rites, bawdy traditional songs and dances and the urbane 'heathen' proclamations of Summerisle's hereditary lord, played by Christopher Lee.

First-time director Robin Hardy makes some predictable low budget choices: sudden zooms, tight close-ups and odd angles. But the apparently simple plot line belies a truly astonishing climax. The power of the surprise creates a nice sympathy between the audience and Howie. Just as his character has underestimated the intelligence of the islanders, so too have the viewers underestimated the power of the film.

Some consider it a horror film because, lets face it, where there is Christopher Lee there's horror. But *The Wicker Man* actually plays out as a lighthearted albeit sturdy mystery (written as it was by *Sleuth* playwright Anthony Shaffer). Thus the ending is all the more a surprise because the shift is so sudden, and so drastically overwhelms the levity it had sustained throughout. Likewise, Edward Woodward maintains a quiet dignity and understated power, right until he meets the wicker man, making his reaction all the more profound.

The masterstroke of the ending is thematic as well. Both cultures win. In traditional cinematic convention, the Islanders have bested Woodward. But within the context of Christian conviction and the legacy of Christian narratives, Woodward's character achieves the ultimate victory.

In the island's pagan tradition everyone sings, which interjects it a hint of Taoist give-and-take; yes Britt Ekland appears naked, but she also sings. That is not to say the song itself is all that bad – check out the band *Lamb*'s 1999 cover of 'Lullaby'.

British Lion's efforts to bury *The Wicker Man* ultimately brought the film greater fame. A new DVD package restores most of the missing footage, shows how *The Wicker Man* was mis-marketed as a horror film and tracks the studio errors that nearly destroyed it altogether.

It's a cult classic because of its unforgettable ending, erotic imagery and general unavailability to the public.

▶▶

WILLY WONKA AND THE CHOCOLATE FACTORY

Date:	1971
Director:	Mel Stuart
Writer(s):	Roald Dahl and David Seltzer (uncredited)
Runtime(s):	100 minutes
Country:	US
Language:	English

IT'S EVERYBODY'S NON-POLLUTIONARY, ANTI-INSTITUTIONARY, PRO-CONFECTIONERY FACTORY OF FUN!

Let me see if this illustrates the deeply held beliefs people have about this film. A huge commotion just erupted here in an LA café where I regularly come to work on this book. Everyone here knows me and asks which film I am doing on a given day. When I said *Willy Wonka and the Chocolate Factory*, the son of one of the workers, an 8-year-old boy, said he had never heard of it. The unanimous response of those within earshot, aged from 8 to 72, was an emphatic, 'He has to see it! Now!' Consequently a group of relative strangers has just rushed him across the street with all the urgency of a blood transfusion, and collectively rented it for him. This in the world's most impersonal and self-absorbed city.

And why shouldn't we love this film. It's a surreal, quasi-psychedelic, gorgeously non-politically-correct, modern Grimm fairy tale. Based on the book *Charlie and the Chocolate Factory* by Roald Dahl, it was made in the days when it was okay to frighten the kids a little (not through violence, but through psychedelic

194

disorientation and uncertainty). Every time I watch children acting rudely and adults doing nothing, I want to rent a C-130 military transport plane and carpet bomb America coast-to-coast with video copies of *Willy Wonka*.

Peter Ostrum is wonderfully sweet as Charlie Bucket. The consummate character actor Jack Albertson is also wonderful as Grandpa Joe, who tells Charlie stories of the goings on down the road at the ultra-secretive Wonka chocolate factory. The film's location is a pan-NATO amalgam, set in a weird nowhere-land placed in time and space between pre-industrial America, Great Britain in the 1950s and nineteenth-century Europe. There's a bizarre mix of architecture, accents, road signs and dialects – wherever the Bucket family live, it's probably the most cosmopolitan small town in the world.

Wonka then announces a worldwide contest. Five golden tickets are hidden in five chocolate bars and the lucky people who find them get a once-in-a-lifetime tour of Wonka's factory. The first four children who find them obviously don't deserve them. Every one of the children is a reflection of parental indulgence, negligence or both. Augustus Gloop (Michael Bollner) is a compulsive eater, Veruca Salt (Julie Dawn Cole) is a spoilt brat, Violet Beauregarde (Denise Nickerson) is an obsessive gum chewer and Mike Teevee (Paris Themmen) is obsessed with TV. Incidentally Mike Teevee from Arizona has one of my favourite lines in all movies when he complains, 'Dad won't let me have a gun', which is qualified with, 'Not till you're 12 son'.

When it turns out the fifth ticket claim is a fraud (the hoaxer is portrayed in newscasts with a photo of Nazi fugitive Martin Bormann), hope springs anew. Charlie Bucket finds it, and he, along with Grandpa Jack, and the other children and parents, enters the factory with a fanfare on the remarkable tour.

It is difficult to do justice to such a wonderfully visual film in print. I will leave it up to you to see it. Even for all its clever conceits and visual tricks the surrealistic core and emotional tenor of this film are all balanced in the performance of Wonka by Gene Wilder. He is magnificent. To see this is to remember just how remarkable Gene Wilder truly is. It was part of a remarkable streak for him: *The Producers* (1968), *Blazing Saddles* (1974), *Young Frankenstein* (1974). I don't think he has diminished; I simply believe roles worthy of him became fewer.

It is a magnificent journey, twisting perception while simultaneously instilling stridently traditional lessons of ethics, decency and health. Not only does the film stand up against the passage of time, it is more vital and necessary than ever. Every bit of recent commercial entertainment for children conditions them towards excess and consumption. *Willy Wonka* is broadside against the inclination to condition children to act out of self-interest and immediate gratification. For, to quote Wonka himself, 'So shines a good deed in a weary world.'

▶▶

WITHNAIL AND I

Date:	1987
Director:	Bruce Robinson
Writer(s):	Bruce Robinson
Runtime(s):	107 minutes
Country:	UK
Language:	English

IF YOU DON'T REMEMBER THE SIXTIES, DON'T WORRY – NEITHER DID THEY.

Relying less on plot than on characterisation, *Withnail and I* is perhaps one of the most quotable films around. One could say that this film is a cult classic based on the dialogue and the performances (Richard E. Grant in particular) alone. To some, that is enough – particularly UK students who often focus on the debauched excesses of the film, having even created a variety of drinking and smoking games around it. Others focus on thematic elements. In America it has become a cult classic among actors, artists and any other arrested adolescents.

By virtue of a greater obscurity in the US, those who are aware of *Withnail and I* tend to take it more seriously and treasure it as a rare find. Therein lies the beauty of this film; you can look at it as deeply as you like or you can look at it as a film about a couple of alcoholics going on a drinking spree to the countryside. *Withnail and I* is a classic on both levels, on both sides of the Atlantic.

It is the tale of a fading, outlived friendship set against the backdrop of a fading, outlived decade of phenodihydro-chloride benelux, old suits, uncontaminated urine and the

'Camberwell carrot'. In Camden,1969, two unemployed actors, Withnail (Richard E. Grant) and 'I' (Paul McGann), are facing the harsh reality of an empty liquor cabinet and the comedown following a speed binge. Squalid living conditions and the prospect of life on the poverty line leads 'I' (also known as Marwood), to suggest a rejuvenating break in the English countryside. After Withnail manages to 'persuade' his flamboyant and eccentric Uncle Monty (Richard Griffiths) to part with the keys of his Lake District cottage, the duo head off for a taste of country life.

Adapting to such an alien environment initially proves difficult for Withnail ('We've gone on holiday by mistake!'), and his predicament is significantly worsened following an altercation with the local poacher, Jake (Michael Elphick). Meanwhile, Marwood is forced to concentrate his attentions on fending off the advances of the lecherous Monty, who has shown up uninvited.

Following an awkward evening, the pair hurriedly return to London and find their bathtub occupied by 'Presuming Ed' (Eddie Tagoe) and the front room appropriated by local drug-dealer/philosopher, Danny (Ralph Brown).

Withnail and I is a very authentic and believable film. Despite a low budget, Robinson manages to bring the late 1960s to life, with no small part played by the soundtrack.

Richard E. Grant has never come close to his performance as Withnail, and plays pissed (in both the UK and US definitions of the word) as well as anyone. Richard Griffith's overbearing, predatory and sexually tormented Uncle Monty is painfully sad, and strangely sympathetic. Ralph Brown is hilarious as the quintessential drug dealer Danny. With so many broad characters, I think Paul McGann is generally underrated for a very generous, understated and steady performance as 'I'.

There has been much said about the homosexual references in this film; I'm sure many believe Withnail and 'I' have some kind of repressed desire. Honestly there really appears to be no discernable sexuality to either Withnail or 'I', as they are too far gone on too many substances to have much libido. It seems to me what they share is a repressed friendship, which is finally and movingly realised when Marwood leaves Withnail at the end of the film. Withnail is a tragic figure who is unlikely to cope on his own.

Early in the film Uncle Monty declares, 'it is the most shattering experience of a young man's life when he awakes and quite reasonably says to himself "I will never play the Dane." When that moment comes, one's ambition ceases.' The line initially seems throwaway until the epic nature of Withnail's ending soliloquy from *Hamlet*. Up to the last scene we've assumed Withnail is out-of-work because he is a bad actor; but we come to realise that he has talent, it's just that alcohol and self-loathing have robbed him of the ability to use it. In American cinema all failure is deserved and all talent eventually rewarded – the underlying conceit being that the system is somehow fair and just. The courage of this complex portrayal is perhaps the most gloriously English aspect of *Withnail and I*.

When *Withnail and I* was first released, I viewed it as a student and laughed very hard. When I viewed it as an out of work artist pushing 30, I cried.

▶▶

INDEX

Soren McCarthy is a performer, writer, freelance journalist and award-winning essayist for National Public Radio. He has written for and appeared in numerous television shows and theatre productions. He lives in New York.